FRINK

FRINK

A PORTRAIT

EDWARD LUCIE-SMITH

AND

ELISABETH FRINK

BLOOMSBURY

Frontispiece shows Elisabeth Frink *c.* 1964—5, photographed by Edward Pool

First published in Great Britain 1994
Bloomsbury Publishing Limited, 2 Soho Square, London W1V 5DE

A CIP catalogue record for this book
is available from the British Library

ISBN 0 7475 1572 7

10 9 8 7 6 5 4 3 2 1

Jacket designed by Sarah Maxey
Text designed by Sarah Maxey and Penny Edwards

Typeset by Hewer Text Composition Services, Edinburgh
Printed by Butler & Tanner Limited, Frome and London

CONTENTS

Introduction	1
I	4
II	30
III	42
IV	58
V	90
VI	104

INTRODUCTION

This is not the book that Elisabeth Frink and I intended to write. Our original plan was for a seamless collaboration, a book which would be entirely in her voice and which would give her viewpoint as a person and as an artist. My role, and I was content with it, would be that of facilitator: I would enable her to say what she wanted to say, arranging and polishing thoughts and words that still remained essentially her own. Our plan was aborted by her illness, and the book is therefore made up of a series of longer and shorter texts which are authentically Frink, always in her own words, as nearly as I can report them, though sometimes pieced together from numerous fragments. The rest is my own linking commentary.

The source for Frink's text is a series of tape-recordings made over a period of about two years. All were made after her illness declared itself. Bouts of illness were responsible for quite numerous interruptions in her work, as was the pressure of other things she had to do. Towards the end of her life one overriding imperative was to finish her huge *Risen Christ* for Giles Gilbert Scott's Anglican cathedral in Liverpool. This, the largest figure she had ever undertaken, was completed and installed on the very eve of her death. Even the final touches, done after the sculpture's return from the foundry, were Frink's own, though she was too ill to attend the actual unveiling.

Our tape-recordings were always made at Frink's house at Woolland, Dorset. I would go there to stay, generally for a couple of days at a time, and we would record as other demands on her time permitted, and also as her declining physical strength allowed. It was seldom that we did more than half an hour at a time, though we might do several such half-hours in the course of a working day. Even if she was not called away to attend to something else, her voice

In the studio at Woolland, *c.* 1990.

1

would generally begin to fail after a short time. Her cancer affected her throat, and if we tried to continue too long she would become almost voiceless. Even so, it was nearly always I, not she, who suggested that the moment had come to take a break. Getting the book finished, even though it obviously took a lower priority than getting the big *Christ* finished, was all part of her fight against the disease which had so unexpectedly attacked her.

As will be seen from some of the things she has to say here, she never accepted that cancer would win in the end. She was determined to fight, though she never deceived herself about her situation. One telling aspect of our conversations was that she was always readier to talk about plans for the future than to reminisce about the past. Every memory, every anecdote about what she had done or thought previously was apt to lead directly to some plan for the future – descriptions of what she wanted to do, as soon as she was fit enough. There is a whole perspective of new projects in this book: images she meant to push further, sculptures she intended to make. Among the things she had in mind were new versions of the *Riace* bronzes – paraphrases on two fifth-century B.C. Greek bronze warriors found in the sea off southern Italy – plus an extension of her *Green Man* series, which was now to include a full-length figure. She also wanted to make a group showing a seated man with a baboon. None of these plans came to fruition, though ambitious drawings for the man-and-baboon group survive. The *Risen Christ* was the conclusion of her career, not the new beginning she willed it to be.

The original tape-recordings are intensely evocative of the setting in which they were made, something which made them correspondingly difficult to transcribe. The transcriptions are therefore my own, not those of a typist. Frink's voice – often, as I have explained, faint in itself – is overlaid with ambient sounds – birds singing, dogs barking, the occasional cackle of poultry, the buzzing of a mower or of a light aircraft overhead. Also, all too frequently, the insistent ringing of the telephone, invariable prelude to an interruption.

None of the places where we conversed was particularly private. Two favourite spots were the terrace beside the swimming pool and the studio, a light, pavilion-like structure close to the main house, whose occupants were clearly visible from the garden, as its walls were almost entirely made of glass. Frink emphasised the fact that making art was a private process and that she disliked being watched when she was at work. Woolland House, nevertheless, had something of the air of a medieval manor, in which life was always, to some extent at least, lived in public. This, in turn, reflected two things – Frink's acceptance, and even enjoyment, of the fact that she was, in addition to being an artist, the manager of a fairly large household which was at the same time a self-contained business enterprise; and her natural sense of hospitality. When Frink described herself as being essentially a countrywoman, this was one of the qualities contained within her self-description. She was quite insistent that making art was only one of a number of activities she enjoyed. If she was in any way unusual as a woman artist it was in her capacity for simultaneously enjoying and managing with competence a busy domestic routine. She never felt that the rituals of domesticity had to be sacrificed to her work as a sculptor.

Many successful contemporary artists now equip themselves with a small crowd of hangers-on – assistants and so-called business managers on the one hand, and on the other muses of different genders. In fact the chief function of all these, however described, seems to be to shield the chief creative spirit from the intrusions of an importunate public, while at the same time providing ego-massage. There were none of these parasites at Woolland. There was instead a constant flow of guests of all kinds – old friends, family members, people there on technical business (from one of Frink's bronze foundries, for instance), collectors and dealers. Even at a time when neither Frink nor her husband Alex Csáky was in good health, all these people were made effortlessly welcome. Delicious meals were served at the long dining table which occupied much of the main room; no one was made to feel out of place or in the way.

It is this atmosphere that no simple transcription of Frink's words can hope to reflect, and that is my reason for attempting to describe it here. What is on the tapes is, in the most literal sense, the echo of a way of life; and it is within the context of this way of life that both Frink's personality and her achievement as a sculptor are to be understood. Many people remarked of Elisabeth Frink that, especially for an artist, hers seemed an unusually open and straightforward nature. In the broad sense, this is true. Yet her personality was certainly complex in a creative sense. I believe that some of its complexities are accurately recorded in what follows.

I

Elisabeth Frink came from the old upper middle class. At the time of her birth, in November 1930, this group was defined more clearly by social attitudes, type of education and choice of profession than by actual possession of money. In her case, the grouping can be defined more narrowly. She came from that part of the upper middle class which had intimate links with the formation and fate of the old British Empire. Her father's family had ties with the former British colonies in North America, and more tenuous ones with the West Indies. Her mother's family served the Raj — the Empire in India. This background was like that of a number of British writers of the late-nineteenth and early-twentieth centuries: the one who comes most immediately to mind is Kipling.

As with many of those who served the Empire, both sides of her family had a high proportion of Celtic, that is to say Scottish and Irish, rather than purely English blood. In addition, the Frinks could claim ancestors who were Dutch and German Protestants, and they had, in addition, some French Huguenot connections. Although she was brought up a Catholic, Frink was to discover the reality of the latter claim during the period she spent in France.

Despite the apparent exoticism of this background, it was also important that Frink's father's family were solidly rooted in Suffolk. Her Suffolk upbringing affected her in different ways. She was born just soon enough to enjoy the last golden age of English country-house life. The childhood pleasures of the 1930s she describes are those which would also have been enjoyed by upper middle-class children of a much earlier generation. Listening to her account of them, we are close to the world not of Kipling but of Trollope.

Yet if Frink's childhood was an idyll, it was an idyll of a rather curious kind, because so much of it was overshadowed by the Second World War. The open Suffolk

With two *Desert Quartet* heads (back view), 1989.

countryside was ideal territory for the great air-bases of Bomber Command. Here, Frink describes briefly the impression the aircraft and their pilots made on her. Elsewhere she cites this wartime experience as one of several sources for the imagery of birds and birdmen which dominates her early work.

The war was significant for her in other ways as well. It meant the prolonged absence of her much-admired soldier father. This may have lain at the root of her lifelong preoccupation with heroic masculine imagery. It also led, during a stay in Dorset before her father left for service overseas, to her first really serious brush with the idea of art as a professional activity. Her rapid transition from the idea of making art in the way that children do, without forethought or afterthought, to a much more considered and self-conscious approach remained mysterious even to her. The two things which can be said are that it took place very early and with remarkably little struggle; and that the few art lessons she was given in Dorset by a young conscientious objector seem to have precipitated it.

Soon after the war ended, her aesthetic development was much accelerated, as she says, by the good luck of a long visit to northern Italy. This took place at a time when most people, certainly most British civilians, were still unable to travel. The great works of art Frink saw in Venice were catalysts which made their presence felt at just the right moment, at a time when her imagination was already excited by things she had seen illustrated in books.

In this sense, Frink belonged to a transitional generation. Direct encounters with masterpieces such as Verrocchio's equestrian statue of the condottiere *Bartolommeo Colleoni, which stands in front of the church of SS Giovanni e Paolo in Venice, were sufficiently rare to remain wholly memorable. On the other hand, Frink's sensibility was already starting to be affected by the availability of lavishly illustrated books on art. She had had access to some of these at her convent boarding-school. As such, she was an early visitor to what André Malraux was later to call the* musée imaginaire. *This non-existent yet wholly visible institution was to haunt her imagination throughout her life.*

My father's family were partly Canadian, but Frink was originally a Dutch Huguenot name, also German. The Frinks went to America and Canada at the time of the persecution of the Huguenots, but first they went to England (there are Frinks in Cornwall), and after that they went across the Atlantic. There are

Elisabeth Frink's Chelsea studio, *c.* 1951. Visible to the left is *Christ at the Column* (destroyed). Propped on the floor is the drawing *Man with Bird* (page 30).

Frinks all up and down the east coast of America and of Canada. My grandfather came from the Canadian branch of the family. By that time they were well-to-do; they'd made money in the insurance business. So they sent him to school in England – we're talking about the turn of the century. He was sent to Sherborne, of all places, and from there he went to Cambridge.

He liked England so much that, apart from going away on holidays, he never actually went back to Canada. He settled down in Suffolk where he married a very nice woman who was partly Irish. Her father had been the Bishop of Barbados at one point. My grandfather had hoped to be a parson, but he had the most terrible stammer, so he became a crammer instead, coaching boys for their examinations. And at the same time he became a typical English country gentleman. The only interruption was the 1914–18 war, when he joined the Staffordshire Regiment and survived Gallipoli.

My father was born at his house in Suffolk, and later on so was I, and then my brother.

My mother is Irish and Scots – she met my father in India. My father was in the army, and since he was a very good horseman he was sent out there as a riding instructor, to a place called Saugar. My mother's father was then the colonel of Skinner's Horse, a very famous Anglo-Indian cavalry regiment. Dad joined them as a young officer, and married the colonel's daughter. My mother was one of those unfortunate children who had to spend years away from their parents because they were in India. She was sent home to a boarding-school in Bexhill at a very early age, and until she was nine she was utterly miserable. Then she was sent to a marvellous woman who took in children whose parents were abroad, and that gave her some kind of family life. That woman later became my godmother.

After spending some time as a boarder at a convent, my mother returned to India when she was sixteen. She used to ride wild horses – all the polo ponies. And that was when she met my father. They got married out there, and had their honeymoon on one of those extraordinary river trips, up in Kashmir. As she says, she sat on a rock for two weeks, three weeks, and watched my father fish – and that was their honeymoon.

When she was twenty-one they came back to England to live, and based themselves at my grandfather's house in Suffolk. But since my father was still

Frink's studio in the 1950s.

in the army, they led a very peripatetic life. During my childhood I went to a number of different schools, wherever Dad was: in Aldershot, in Scotland, then back in Aldershot again. However, I was born in Suffolk, and the house there is what I remember best. It was a marvellous place to be because it was a great old country house, nothing terribly special – stucco outside – but a nice old country house with enormous attics which were fantastic for children. We used to climb up into them, and there were always boxes of old clothes we could dress up in.

One of my earliest memories is of the time I nearly drowned. In fact, I'm never quite sure if I do remember it, or whether it's because the story has been told to me so often. It's such a vivid picture. We had a fish pond, a lily pond, in front of the house, and I was trying to get something out of it. I was two and a half, and I fell in. I remember being dragged out – or this is what I think I remember – and I also remember seeing my nurse leaning out of one of the top windows with her mouth wide open. And everybody was shouting. After they pulled me out I was taken upstairs and thrown into a bath of hot water – we still had hip baths at that time. And apparently it was just in the nick of time.

For five years I was on my own till my brother was born, but I had a lot of friends, little friends who used to come and play – in the attics, and in the gardens and orchards. I went to the village school to start with, so I had friends in the village. And at the age of three I was given my own pony. What I liked was the outdoors. I didn't like dolls – I was a very physical child. I liked rather boyish things: guns and soldiers' uniforms and things like that. Though I didn't mind being dressed up in a pretty party dress – we always dressed up when we went to parties, and played all those wonderful old-fashioned children's games. But best of all I liked being out of doors, because of riding, and because of the dogs. One of my vivid memories is of skating on the lakes. The winters in Suffolk were always terribly cold. Another is of fireworks at night. After my brother got a little older, he used to have his own gang in the village, and I used to join them.

The really big drama of my childhood was the war, which started when I was nine. My father was at Dunkirk, and for some time we didn't know if he was OK – he was one of the last to be picked up. But anyway, he got out. After that he was in Aldershot again, then we went to Dorset for a few months. That was my first sight of Dorset, which I now love very much. We stayed on the coast

Apocalypse, drawing (1950). Frink had been making drawings of this type even earlier; she exhibited some of them at Heffer's bookshop in Cambridge – her first public appearance as an artist.

10

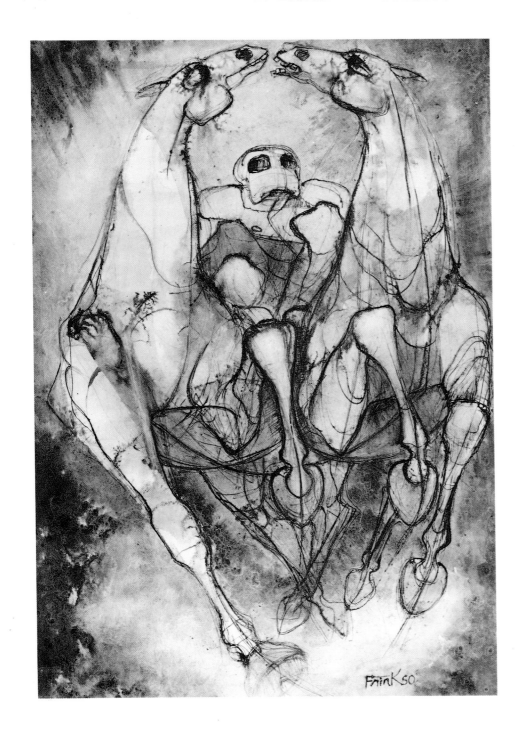

near Corfe Castle in order to be near my father. I began to be quite interested in drawing when we stayed in Dorset. We stayed with a family, and their son was at home because he was a conscientious objector — of course, everyone mumbled about it. He was called Roddy, and he was very sensitive — a painter. He taught me: he gave me big sheets of paper and watercolours, and I began to splash paint on. I'd never done that as a younger child. When I was small, I only used to make rather niggly little pencil drawings — animals and horses and birds — nothing imaginative at all. I think it was Roddy who got me going. I started doing some quite interesting things — slightly Gothic, a bit Germanic. I think I'd seen some German art in a book — perhaps Grünewald — which rather impressed me. I did rather apocalyptic drawings: men on skeleton horses, things like that. I started doing those at a definite time, between the ages of twelve and fourteen; I've still got one or two of them.

After our time in Dorset my father went off abroad. We didn't really see him again properly until the end of the war. He was sent out to India, with a regiment which finally ended up in Burma. So my mother was entirely alone throughout the war. She thought of sending us, my brother and me, to relations in Canada, but in the end she didn't, something for which I'm profoundly thankful, quite apart from the fact that a lot of those boats with evacuees were sunk. I went to school at a convent in Devon, but always came home for the school holidays. I still lived a very physical existence. I had been taught to shoot by my father, and I used to go out and shoot rabbits — that was quite useful, it gave us something for the pot. I used to shoot across the fields, and was very much a loner. A loner in the sense that I wanted to be alone. Despite the fact that my father was away, we had a very good family life, because my mother looked after us all. She kept us together, and meanwhile she looked after my grandfather, who had become an absolutely impossible old man. She must have been under a considerable strain, with Dad away fighting. But there were a lot of family friends about, people with children, so I wasn't bereft of company if I wanted it.

During that time I read a lot. I graduated from Grimm's fairy-tales and Hans Christian Andersen to *The Scarlet Pimpernel* (I had a craze for him), and for books by Georgette Heyer. After that I graduated to more serious novels. My mother always encouraged us to read.

In her studio, early 1960s. The group *Assassins II* (1963) is on the floor.

12

13

14

I had a great admiration for men from an early age. This was partly because my father was extremely handsome. I was used to meeting all his colleagues – his fellow officers – and they were very glamorous in their uniforms: cavalry boots and things like that. Men were very much part of my early life because of the army. I used to look up to them, and hero-worship them. By contrast I found boys of my own age rather tedious, though I would still rush round the village with my brother's gang.

In Suffolk during the war there was a whole bunch of very jolly Polish airmen who used to come to the house. My mother made them feel very much at home. They'd sit around and drink a lot of vodka and be very noisy. Then they'd go off in their flying machines – and sometimes they got killed. We were right next door to an operational aerodrome, and sometimes we'd see the planes coming home on fire.

I enjoyed school by that time. I was taught French by French nuns, and I also had some very good art lessons. Very traditional teaching. I was taught to draw – plaster casts, bowls of fruit, exercises in perspective. I think I was very lucky because the art teacher had a lot of books. I was able to learn the basics about the different schools of painting.

Music also meant quite a lot to me. My mother had a collection of records – symphonies, operas and concertos – and we used to put those on and listen together. Her father, my maternal grandfather, also had a wonderful collection of records. We used to go and stay with him sometimes. But on army pay there was no extra money for music lessons. It was that or art.

When my father came back from the Burma campaign, after the end of the war against Japan, he was given command of a regiment out in Trieste. We went out there in 1947, to join him for a Christmas holiday. We went on an army train, and my brother and I were separated, because boys and girls were put in different carriages. I was supposed to keep an eye on him, but of course I didn't. Just as we were going into Austria the train started to go at blinding speed. It turned out later that the guards at the back were actually sitting on the brakes, trying to slow the train down. The train-driver was drunk, absolutely drunk. I looked out of the window at Klagenfurt, and this bundle fell out of the engine-driver's place, and there was a cascade of green bottles in the snow.

I had a remarkable time in Italy because my mother was free to take us

Frink with *Female Torso* (1954–5), one of her rare depictions of the female figure. The piece remained uncast until 1982.

15

Frink in the early 1960s.

children where we wanted to go. My brother went back to school, but I stayed on because I fell off a horse and got concussion very badly. It was quite an experience being near Trieste. There were these huge balls that the army threw. I was allowed to go to those; my mother made me a ball dress. I also went to my first opera. It was *Cav. and Pag.*, with Tito Gobbi. The most important thing, however, was that my mother and I went to Venice. We stayed at the Daniele, which was wonderful then. It was the most astonishing experience for me — because of the war nobody of my generation had had the opportunity to go abroad and see great works of art in their proper setting. The city was very cold and misty. We went to see the glass-blowers in Murano, and the dungeons in the Doge's Palace. But we also saw the Accademia and the Colleoni statue. All these things suddenly came to life for me: the paintings and the sculptures. When I finally came home, to do my School Certificate back with the nuns, it was very difficult.

Unlike many artists, Frink met no opposition from her parents concerning her choice of career. They had already received some proof, when her drawings were exhibited at Heffer's bookshop in Cambridge, that she was likely to be exceptionally gifted.

The art world she entered as a student was very different from the art world as it exists today. Art was not the great international industry it has now become. Attitudes in British art schools remained conservative. Even the influence of the Bauhaus was felt only in a rather diluted form. As Frink points out, major exhibitions of twentieth-century art were still few and far between. Nevertheless, even in Britain, the whole process which legitimated contemporary art had already begun. The founders of Modernism — artists such as Matisse and Picasso — were among the major beneficiaries of the Second World War. By an ironic paradox, Nazi opposition to "degenerate art" gave Modernism the final push which made it respectable.

I started at art school very soon after I left the convent. I wanted to do art, and I didn't want to do anything else, and my parents were happy to let me. They chose Guildford because my father wasn't very well. He came back from Burma with something he'd caught there, which wasn't detected at the time, and he had to go to a sanatorium for a year. My mother wanted to be near him, and Guildford was convenient. I was there for eighteen months, and it turned out to be a good place to start. We were very well taught. I thought I was going to do painting, but I very quickly switched to sculpture because Trevor Tennant, who ran the department, decided I had more aptitude for that. We used clay and we were also taught to carve. I did quite a few castings in that black cement. That gave me a great sense of achievement: getting out of the clay and into a cast.

Guildford School of Art was very good, in the sense that I discovered doing sculpture there. But you had to do an awful lot of other things as well. You had architecture, costume, furniture down the ages, anatomy, life drawing. I found all that very boring, apart from anatomy and life drawing, which I liked very much. It seemed an awful lot to cram into one year. There was no interest in abstract art, apart from some information about it in the history of art classes, which were quite an important part of the course. In fact, for us, abstract art, in the practical sense, or even in the intellectual sense, just didn't exist. We didn't even discuss it, unless we happened to go to an exhibition which featured it. And there weren't many of those at that time.

Nevertheless, when Frink moved to London, to become a student at Chelsea School of Art, the world she inhabited, and which she describes so vividly here, still had a lingering flavour of the nineteenth century. In many respects it was not so different from the world described in Henri Murger's novel La Vie de Bohème, *now most vividly preserved for us in the opera Puccini derived from it. It was a life of simple, rather rumbustious pleasures, lived for the most part in one fairly small quarter of London, the area around the King's Road which had long been the traditional haunt of artists.*

After Guildford I moved to London and went to Chelsea, where I'd won a small scholarship. My first year in London was a nightmare because I lived with a family who were old friends of my parents. At the age I was then, it was thought I probably needed a certain amount of supervision. I was miles away, in Golders Green in north London, which was just awful, because I had to trail up there every night. If I had a late supper in Chelsea, I still had to go all the way up there afterwards. The woman I was staying with always insisted on leaving me dinner, no matter what. I'd have to tip it in the dustbin, so she'd think I'd eaten it. Later, I moved to Chelsea itself and lived there, mostly in various rooms in Oakley Street — a great many of those houses in Oakley Street were let out in rooms. At one time seven

Top: In France, late 1960s.
Above: With her mother, Jean, late 1960s.

17

of us shared a flat in the King's Road, where we used to throw parties.

We all had a marvellous time, even though none of us had any money. There were parties at least once a week – not only students, but senior members of staff. We used to have the annual art-school picnic. Several bus-loads of us would go down to Sonning or Cookham-on-Thames – some place on the river: it was a real, traditional school outing. We used to go to the Chelsea Arts Ball. We made a float, and all of us dressed up. The best year was when we went as mermaids, with nothing on underneath some netting. That was great fun – though I also remember that everyone used to get extremely drunk and overturn the floats, despite the fact that they had quite a lot of bouncers around who were meant to stop them. When I went as a mermaid I had to be rescued by a very nice Welshman, who stopped me from being completely trampled underfoot by some ghastly monster.

Everyone who knew Elisabeth Frink at that time remembers her as an extraordinarily attractive girl. Much of the attraction is preserved in photographs, and also in the full-length portrait sculpture made by her friend F. E. McWilliam. A cast of this stood in the entrance courtyard at Woolland. Inevitably her life was not without its sentimental complications.

There were groups of older students at both Guildford and Chelsea, people out of the services who were coming back to civilian life, whom we all rather looked up to and admired, or even fell in love with from a distance, because they seemed rather dashing, being older and having been in the war. I always used to fall for older men, funnily enough, rather than for my contemporaries – people who'd been in the war were amazingly glamorous to me. I had lots of boyfriends, but the first really serious one was an ex-fighter pilot who'd had a partial lobotomy. In other words, he was sane some of the time; and some of the time he wasn't sane at all. So I had this extraordinary relationship with a man who was in fact two different people.

Of course my family were extremely worried about this, as most people would be – about what kind of future lay in store if I married a man like this. They were nevertheless wonderful. They said, 'You must do what you think right.' So Arthur and I became engaged. Then fortunately I saw the light, because he was really impossible to live with. For example, I'd come home and

Domestic life *chez* Jammet, *c.* 1955.

19

Frink c. 1957.

In her studio, early 1960s.

find he'd taken my gramophone – the kind of wind-up gramophone we had then – down to the pawnbroker's. He used to have bouts of drinking, serious drinking, and on top of that he was taking some kind of medication for his mental state – a most ferocious thing called paraldehyde. I used to find that most of my belongings had been popped, or even vandalised, which I didn't so much mind. Life nevertheless became quite untenable, so we parted company. So much to everyone's relief, including my own, I didn't marry him. I was only twenty-one when I knew Arthur, and rather immature, I think, for my age.

In general, Frink recalled this period with relish, but also with a vivid sense of its restrictions and privations. Though she had not yet paid her first visit to Paris, the lifestyle, and even the style of dress, which she describes were very similar to those of the contemporary Existentialists of Saint-Germain-des-Prés. Though jeans had already become a universally acceptable form of dress in bohemian circles, London had not felt the full impact of the new American ways. In the early 1950s the British art world, in particular, still looked across the Channel, rather than across the Atlantic.

People did used to get extraordinarily drunk – I don't know if they do so much, nowadays. Pot hadn't arrived. We used to drink rough cider and beer mainly, and then if we had a party we used to mix the whole lot up together. The only wine which was available then was pretty awful Algerian stuff, which was very bad for the stomach.

The King's Road in those days was still a village – it really was. All our digs and rooms were usually very small, and not very nice. Dreadful meters for everything, and those Ascot heaters which blew up when you wanted a bath. Very often kitchens used to have the bath at one end, with a board over the top. So you didn't exactly want to hang around at home. You spent your evenings in the pub, or else at a jazz club. We also used to go to the cinema a lot, and sometimes to the theatre. As I grew older I came to love the Royal Court. Most of our amusements were in Chelsea itself. We saw a great many French films, for instance, because you got them at the Chelsea Classic. The only thing you had to move out of Chelsea for was jazz. When you wanted to listen to that you had to go up to Oxford Street or Soho. There were little clubs in Chelsea, but they were mainly drinking clubs.

21

We were all extremely poor. A few of us had grants – I had a grant for a bit, from Suffolk. And my mother and father gave me an allowance, as much as they could. But they didn't really have any money because army pay was pretty abysmal then. My grandfather had enough to live on comfortably in Suffolk, but not enough to give away. I used to do life-class modelling to make money. I'd go to St Martin's School of Art and strip off, and I'd go to the Royal College. It was extremely hard work: usually you were freezing cold on one side, and boiling hot on the other. But it was always interesting to see what other people made of you.

As students we all lived on about five pounds a week, including rent. You didn't eat enormously well on that, unless you were taken out to dinner at a nice restaurant. I don't think any of us did much cooking in my student days – we just used to brew something up. I don't remember cooking at all until I got married. Then I married a Frenchman, so I learned the hard way.

We weren't particularly into clothes, either. In fact, we were fed up with them. In those days you just couldn't buy decent clothes. And we were frightened of the New Look fashions with their long skirts. We used to buy jeans and take them apart. Then we'd machine them up again and make them absolutely skin tight, as skin tight as possible. And we'd re-cut T-shirts, which were very badly made anyway. Loose tops and very tight trousers are what I seem to remember as the thing. There were none of those wonderful clothes that young people can buy now. You had to invent ideas for yourself, because what was available was just so awful. Mary Quant was responsible for jazzing all that up, really. When she came on the scene, things started looking up. It was a very grey period for clothes. Yet in a sense it was good fun, doing something to your clothes yourself, to make them more wearable.

Dead Hen, bronze (1956) – purchased by the Tate from an exhibition at the Beaux Arts Gallery when still in plaster, and cast at their expense.

One of the distinguishing marks of Frink's career is the fact that she achieved recognition early. As she soon discovered, this had disadvantages as well as advantages. She found herself classified as a member of a group of sculptors – the immediate successors of Henry Moore – who were all much older than herself. In an increasingly volatile art world, youthful celebrity also carried with it the possibility of early eclipse. This never in fact happened to her: she was too vigorously creative. Yet she was, during the latter part of her career – and indeed from the mid-1960s onwards

24

– keenly conscious of her unsettled position in the hierarchies of the British art world. Although she was the recipient of public honours, among them the DBE, and frequently in demand for important public commissions, her status as an artist remained uncertain, both in her own mind and, it must be said, in those of leading critics and curators. For her a symbol of this was the Tate Gallery's neglect. After making one early purchase, it remained stubbornly indifferent, under a succession of directors, to the possibility of acquiring more of her work.

I'd already had my first London exhibition in 1952, while I was still a student. I got to know Helen Lessore at the Beaux Arts Gallery, and her policy was to put on work by young people, and to help them. I was given a show with three or four others. One was the sculptor Raymond Mason, who now lives and works in Paris; and there was another sculptor called Michael Werner, who died recently. The painters were upstairs and the sculptors downstairs. I had some strange bird shapes on show, and the Tate bought one of these, straight out of this first London exhibition. Everything was still in plaster, so the Tate paid to have a cast made – it was a funny bird, almost abstract. They've never bought anything of mine since then.

That show was the beginning of my reputation as a sculptor. I was regarded as being sort of contemporary with people like Lynn Chadwick, Reg Butler and Kenneth Armitage – though in fact they were somewhat older than me – because we were all showing in the same exhibitions. For a while we were all lumped together as the new school of British sculpture, all angry and angular, and indeed to some extent the idea persists to this day. I think that's really boring. I was, of course, friendly with most of these sculptors, but not particularly close to them personally, because they were all at least ten years older than me. And I don't like all their work equally. For example, while I've always liked Kenneth Armitage's work very much, probably best out of all that group, I never particularly went for Reg Butler's. Butler himself was a very strange man – very difficult to talk to.

Early recognition did not bring with it immediate financial success. Like most British artists of the immediately post-war period – even well-established ones – Frink had to derive a substantial part of her livelihood from teaching. With her open yet forceful personality, and her sensitivity to other people's needs and ideas, she must have been

Two Nude Men, drawing (1950).

very good at the job. Yet she soon found the tide starting to turn against her in the major London art schools where she was employed, and particularly at St Martin's. St Martin's, at the beginning of the 1960s, became the chief command post for a revolution in British sculpture, carried out under the leadership of Anthony Caro, who, in turn, had been inspired by what was taking place in America – in particular by the work of the American sculptor David Smith, and by close personal contact with the leading New York critic Clement Greenberg. Frink was always out of sympathy with purely abstract art, and one of the aims pursued by Caro and his faithful band of followers was to banish all traces of the figurative. She was also repelled by the fact that the new direction in sculpture was so doctrinaire, and so hostile to artists – most of all to students – who wanted to pursue a different path.

I did quite a lot of teaching after I left Chelsea – I did it for fourteen years in all. When I started it was difficult, because I was really almost still a student. I joined the staff at Chelsea, and I felt I was teaching my contemporaries. I felt I was learning as much as they did. Yet I also enjoyed it very much. In addition to the job at Chelsea I had one at St Martin's. I did two days a week there, plus evening classes. And that was nice, because I earned some money. And to begin with St Martin's was enjoyable too. I left when Anthony Caro took over there, and the teaching became dominated by him. I remember that I was teaching there during the time when he was in the States. Then he came back with the gospel, the new idea, and wanted everything to change.

One problem was that I felt all the students should learn to draw, that they should do life drawing at least once a week, and that there should be a model available at all times in the school. And that was no longer so. It was all chucked out, in favour of design studies and all that. It was very funny – when they occasionally had a model at St Martin's, they used to hide her with a box. They were doing their damnedest not to allow any sort of human feeling for the body – it was very strange. In the end I don't think it was very fruitful. Of course it was OK for Caro, because it was his own chosen way. St Martin's developed a prevailing orthodoxy, a very tough one too, and the staff really laid it on the line. Everything else was discouraged. I found that kind of rigidity strange in an art context. After all, during the developing years of Modernism most of the best abstract artists went through the figurative experience. They

In France, late 1960s.

28

all learned to draw from life. The fascinating thing about fashions in art, of course, is that they come round full circle. They reach a certain point, then round they go again.

So how, in fact, do you teach art? I think you can't actually teach it. You can only make suggestions. If you're any sort of teacher at all, you don't tell students what to do, because obviously they must have their own ideas. You can't tell them to do a sculpture of a man running because that's putting ideas into their heads. They have to do imaginative work, their own thing. I think the only thing you can really teach them is how to set a piece of sculpture up so it doesn't fall down. What the best materials are. In art all you can teach is structure – movement and structure. Tensions in the body. And anatomy. Things which are obvious from an anatomical point of view. You try to indicate to them what they should actually look at – the structure of people standing, walking, lying down. The structure of a head. And that of animal forms. I think it's the most you can possibly do. Once you've taught them that, it's over to them.

I think being there, being available for students, is also very important. When you're learning you don't necessarily want to be left on your own. You want to be able to feel that there's someone there for you. 'Can we just talk about what I'm doing?' I think that's very important.

However, I think collective discussions are an American thing. I got very bored with them when I went to Skowhegan. The painters' groups and sculptors' groups were so busy discussing they didn't even bother to look at the work of art. By contrast, teaching one to one is very rewarding. It was very good for me – I learned a lot on my side. I learned how to put my thoughts into words.

I think when I was teaching things were somewhat different from the way things are now. When I was a teacher, it was all very strict. Now I think students have much more freedom. And, now I think about it, they're probably much more serious. I do get a lot of students coming down here to Woolland, and I always try to make time for them. They want to know how I work; they want to look at sculpture. It's always interesting what they ask you, though occasionally I meet some who haven't done any homework at all. I try to encourage them to ask questions of their own which are not simply connected with my CV.

With a *Goggle Head*, France, 1969.

30

II

Frink was more inclined to reminisce about the very earliest part of her career than about her middle and later years. She would not, I think, have felt that a detailed account of her second and third marriages had any place in the kind of book we planned. She was willing to talk about her first marriage (which lasted from 1955 to 1963) because of its impact on her work. By taking her frequently to Ireland, where her French husband's family had settled, it aroused an interest in buried Celtic roots. There is in fact quite an intimate link between some of her most typical imagery and primitive Celtic art and religion. In particular, she was aware of the parallel between her own obsession with the human head, as a kind of vessel into which various ideas and emotions could be poured, and the Celtic cult of the head.

I was introduced to an Irishman – I forget his name now, was it Desmond something? – who was very jolly and came to several of our parties. He said he was going back to Ireland and invited me to come too. So I decided to go. When I arrived in Dublin, he met me, but was obviously rather embarrassed. I think he'd thought I wouldn't take up the invitation. He had an Irish girlfriend who was extremely put out that I had arrived. So he had to do everything he could to keep me amused. The best ploy, from his point of view, was to introduce me to some other people, friends of his. One of the men he produced was Michel Jammet, who was to become my first husband. When we got together, that sorted Desmond's problem out.

The Jammets were an extremely interesting French family, living in Dublin. Michel was an architect, working there, but his family owned the famous Jammet's Restaurant, an absolutely wonderful French place, started by his grandfather, in Nassau Street. During the war, it was the only place in Dublin

Man with Bird, drawing (1951) – visible in an early photograph of Frink's Chelsea studio (page 6).

31

where you could get decent meals. Michel was the second son, and his younger brother now ran the restaurant with their father. They were a fascinating, marvellous family.

After we got married we used to spend a lot of holidays in Dublin. I had a very good time getting to know lots of Irish people – one was the poet Patrick Kavanagh. Dublin was in a sense much more barbaric than the Chelsea I knew, really wild. The evenings were the wildest time of all. One used to go beyond the city boundaries, and then you could drink all night.

One thing about Ireland: no matter what happened, at some point in the night everyone would sit down and talk about the Troubles – about what happened four hundred years ago. It was King Billy and the Battle of the Boyne all over again. I think the British did unspeakable things to the Irish, and they've never forgotten. These discussions at the end of the evening impressed me enormously. The Irish are such a strange race: they're so intelligent and artistic and literary. I've always felt there's quite a lot of Celtic feeling in my own sculptures of heads. I did see a lot of Celtic sculpture in Ireland – we travelled about quite a bit. Michel was completely French, but a lot of Irish had rubbed off on him.

The period Frink spent in France in the late 1960s and early '70s has the quality of a self-contained episode. Her decision to go there remained mysterious to many of her friends. It would have been more explicable if she had still been married to her first, French, husband, but the move took place after they were divorced. It helped that she had retained a good command of the French language from her convent schooldays. She also discovered family links with the region of France where she chose to live – but this discovery was made, as she herself says, only after her decision to settle there.

Essentially, and perhaps paradoxically, her move to France was part of her ongoing dialogue with what was then happening in the British art world. In a negative sense, it expressed her disillusionment with the new modes of sculpture then being fostered by Caro and his followers: it was a visible mark of her sense of exclusion. Yet there was also a more positive aspect. The move to France can be read as a declaration of artistic independence. She was now willing to stand completely on her own feet and trust in her own artistic resources. Despite the move, however, her eyes remained firmly fixed on the British art world as the appropriate arena in which

The house in the Cevennes, with Lin Jammet on horseback in French hussar's uniform.

With her son Lin as a baby, *c.* 1958–9.

33

With her first husband, Michel Jammet,
1955.

34

to operate. It is significant that, throughout the whole period of her French residence, she never attempted to hold exhibitions in France.

Originally, the house in France was simply for holidays. We went down to see some friends and found this amazing place for £3,000 and bought it. It was nothing to do with my first marriage – I was already divorced from Michel Jammet. It was really rather ironical that I should be living in France with my British rather than my French husband.

It's a difficult decision to make – to go and live and work in another country – because you cut yourself off: out of sight is out of mind. I made the decision when I was and I wasn't established. Abstract art was very much the new wave in England, and people suddenly seemed to find figurative art very boring. I felt I'd become unpopular with the arts establishment, though there was still a body of collectors who'd always supported my work. But the British Council, for example, had stopped sending my sculptures abroad.

We'd already bought this place in France – that happened in 1964 – and in 1967 it seemed like a good time to move out. I had a feeling I wanted to cut myself off for a while from the British scene. However, the break was never complete. I used to come back regularly to England to go to bronze foundries – I never found a suitable foundry down there, and I also didn't find a gallery: I didn't show in France till latterly. I was working in one country and showing in another.

In many ways the move suited us very well. My son Lin was just at the beginning of his education, and he was half French anyway and already spoke French, so it wasn't a problem for him to switch schools. Yet it was also quite a strange existence. I had to start my studio all over again in a barn, and we never saw anyone in the winters, which were long and cold – you were thrown very much on your own resources. In the summer all our friends screeched down from England.

Obviously there are landmarks in everyone's life, and the period in France turned out to be one of them for me – though I didn't know this when we bought the house. My son went to school locally, and one of his friends was called Robotier. The name seemed familiar somehow. Then I made a visit to England, and was talking to my mother about it. I already knew that part of my

With her second husband, Edward Pool, at their wedding, 1964.

35

family was of Huguenot origin, so we looked at the family tree. And there was the name Robotier. It turned out that the family tree given for the Robotiers in the pedigree my mother had was identical to the one I found in a book I bought about the Robotiers in the Cevennes. Where we all came from was a little château about six miles north of the house we bought in 1964. Finding that out was quite a shock to me in a way.

I discovered that the château now belonged to an antique dealer called Madame Becq. She and I became quite good friends, and I used to tease her about living in my family's house.

However, I never thought that I'd live in France for the rest of my life. Eventually we'd have to come home. One reason that we decided to come back to England in 1973 was that I felt I was getting out of touch.

Though Frink was reticent about her marriages, she was willing to talk candidly about what to many people would seem an even more intimate topic: the fact that she was suffering from cancer. In addition to talking to me about it, for the record, on tape, she gave an interview on the same subject to the London Evening Standard. This formed part of a regular series of interviews with celebrities entitled 'Me and My Health'. The majority of the paper's other interviewees spoke when they were healthy, not when they were ill. Frink's purpose was typically altruistic – she wanted to try and disperse some of the terrible fear which surrounded any mention of the disease which had attacked her.

Frink was an optimist, but also a realist. She was aware that she might not survive, but she was nevertheless determined to do so if she could. It was typical of her approach that, while she was prepared to speak about her illness, she soon turned from the subject of being ill to her many plans for the future once she had succeeded – as she hoped – in recovering completely. In her terms, mere survival would not have been enough. It was what she could do with an additional span of years which concerned her.

Cancer is a disease that everybody dreads, and it's very difficult to come to terms with it because you feel very threatened, you feel totally vulnerable. First you feel stunned, then you've got to come to terms with the fact that, well, you've got it, so what can you do about it?

Well, I was told that of course they could operate and that the operation was

At the house in France, with Edward Pool. The houses were originally designed for silk-weavers.

Bird Man

generally very successful. And it has been successful, but recently they decided to give me radiotherapy because they saw a little shadow that they didn't like. That's the awful thing about cancer: there's always the possibility that it will come back. There's no getting away from it. At the same time you have to be particularly positive-thinking because one knows that people have fought cancer, very serious cancers, and have won simply on sheer spirit, by refusing to allow it to take over. I was talking to a friend the other day who also has cancer and we talked about our various treatments, and he said that of course he hadn't taken any treatment at all. His attitude was totally different from mine. Mine is to fight it on every level and be totally positive about it. I've told it to go away, and that's it, because I want to see my grandson grow up. And he said that he'd decided to say to his cancer, 'Come in and do what you will – live inside me.'

I think being ill and having to get over a major operation was the most shattering thing for me because I've always been extraordinarily fit, and coping with the physical side was very hard. You need a lot of help; you need help all round. Psychologically it's the most terrible blow because there's always the sneaking feeling that whatever you do it may not work out in the end. Yet you've got to accept that it will, otherwise you might as well sit down and die. That sounds very dramatic – but you have to treat it like that. There are days when you think, 'If it's a matter of another couple of years, what shall I do?' I talked to an interesting French doctor, and she said she'd got over an early cancer – she's fine now; she's forty-something. She said, 'You have to accept your death; first you've got to accept the fact that you're going to die. Once you've done that, it becomes easier to fight the disease.' That's an interesting point, if you look at it fair and square and think, 'I might be dead in two years' time.'

At the moment I'm obsessed with the desire to leave the place in reasonable order. I've been tearing up my bad drawings for about a week – that sort of thing. I'd like to leave everything in good shape for my son, so that if he wants the place, he can have it. Apart from that I'm very cheerful. One difficult thing is physical weakness. It's taking me a long time to get my strength back; my muscles have gone completely. People say, 'Well, you've got to rest; you've got to rest every day after lunch.' Which I do, though I find it very hard to accept.

Birdman, drawing (1959).

However, the point is that I feel very enthusiastic about my work, very positive about that – quite excited. I think one of the results of this disease is that you have periods of quite exciting possibilities. I think from that point of view I'm very lucky, because, since I have my work, I have enormous support. I'm not just sitting around trying to get myself fit – I have something to occupy my mind.

At work on *Flying Men* (1982).

III

As will be seen from what follows, Elisabeth Frink had no doubt about her vocation as an artist. She was very content to be what she was, and the whole working process of making sculpture gave her immense satisfaction. Her attitude to what she did in the studio was extremely down to earth and practical, as is evident from her account of the advice she gave to the students who came to see her. Just as in her formal teaching days she spoke not of theory, but about the essential business of getting the figure to stand up.

Though she was a committed Modernist, the processes she describes are still in a broad sense traditional. Despite her preference for plaster rather than clay – she only used clay when making portraits – she built up her sculptures upon an armature in a traditional, quasi-academic way, ready to be cast in bronze. She claimed to dislike making the armature itself, but it is clear that the artisanal, hands-on nature of the process was one of the primary reasons why it gave her great satisfaction.

For Frink, the end product was never a purely formal statement. It was a poetic image, an embodiment of complex thoughts and feelings within herself. One important reason for working so often in series was that she frequently found it impossible to resolve all these thoughts and feelings within the compass of a single piece of sculpture.

If someone says, 'Well, you work so hard,' the answer is, 'I'm only happy when I *am* working.' The irritation is not being able to work, being prevented in some way or other. That's when it really hurts. Being an artist is the most wonderful life because you've chosen to do it, and you can do it. That's the thing I think of most, how lucky I am. Yet one doesn't want to be pompous in saying something like that – 'How lucky I am! What awful lives other people have!' One doesn't

Working outdoors on one of the *Desert Quartet* heads, 1989.

44

know what lives other people have. To me it would be absolutely ghastly to have to go off to a factory every morning.

For me, the important part of the day is the morning. It always has been, since I was much younger. I feel that if I don't start early, I've lost the day. So most of my work is done before lunch, and if I'm really into something demanding then I do a bit more after lunch. I work every day. *Now* I work every day. I think that when I was younger I didn't do that because I was very easily put off. And I suppose one's head was full of so many other things. As you get older you do less, but you do more work because you become much more disciplined and you enjoy it.

I get up, have a swim, have my breakfast and go to the studio around eight, maybe a bit earlier. My mind works well in the morning, and in the evening I do something else — cooking, listening to music, things like that.

I have to put the plaster on and take it off myself. After all, nobody else can do that. People do help me to do my armatures. Making an armature is really building up a skeleton in iron. Whether it's a large one or a small one it's all the same. However, what I always say to students is that you shouldn't tie yourself down too much. The legs of a figure must be where they're going to be — that's rule number one. Move the legs and the figures fall over. They have to be grounded in a very stable manner. But from the pelvis or waist up I treat the figures in quite a free fashion. I build up the thorax and chest in chicken-wire and keep turning it round, so that I see what sort of movement I'm going to have, what inclination of the head. Often I stop and study it for quite a long time. I like freedom of choice. You imagine the sculpture — you see it in your mind's eye, but then of course it escapes you as you build up, and other things happen. It invariably turns out different. The idea may still be there, but the form will have changed enormously. I'm not nearly so precise in the way I work as Henry Moore was. He made maquettes, then made the same thing — pretty much — in a larger size.

I use chicken-wire, and hessian soaked in plaster, which gives a good surface to build on, and then I just pile more plaster on with my hands. I often use sawdust and stuff mixed up with the plaster, which gives a much more gritty texture. Then I correct it as I go along. Right from the beginning I carve it back. It's a constant process of rebuilding and adjusting, of carving back, until

At work on *Running Man I*, 1979.

I've got just what I want. The process is totally flexible — that's one of the marvellous things about working in plaster. Once it has set you have a completely rigid thing to work on, to take to the next stage. It's not like clay, which is always falling apart and dripping. I hate using clay. Quite apart from everything else, it weighs a ton.

Eventually you arrive at a point where in your own terms the sculpture is finished, and the only way you could possibly improve it is to do another one. I find that if I think it might possibly be better to change it in some way, it's better to leave it, and do another variation. In the past I've often broken things up. That's a great nuisance but it's also very satisfactory. You just feel that you've worked your way through something and it hasn't succeeded, so you'd better start again.

More and more I work in series. I've got a capacity for parallel thought. For working on one piece, with another simmering in a different part of my mind. I've done it all my life, and I do it even more often now. In the same way, if I'm cooking I'm also thinking about something else.

I usually feel a new series happening long before I actually do it. I can feel it coming on. For example I heard about the *Riace* figures two or three years before I started doing my own versions. I stack the idea away and draw on it later. For example, the big new dog which I call *Leonardo's Dog*: I first thought of doing that all of four years ago. We were in the Loire Valley, visiting Amboise, and I didn't know that Leonardo had spent his last days in France, and had actually died there. It was a total surprise to me. It just shows how bad my art history is. We discovered Leonardo's house near the château, which had been given to him by François I. In the cellar were models of all his inventions, and outside the door was a wonderful medieval dog, an old stone one with a big collar, chained to the door, very worn. This got me into the idea of doing a seated dog, it started something in my mind.

Frink's insistence on the importance of light, and of the reaction of the sculptural surface to light, in her work may surprise many people. It points to an element which is sometimes overlooked — her position as a direct descendant of Rodin. She said over and over again that Rodin was the first artist, the first major sculptural personality, to make an impact on her.

With a group of *Tribute* heads, late 1970s.

At this point it is worth noting that Rodin's art has two important and in some ways self-contradictory aspects. Because of the restless fluidity of his surfaces, he has sometimes been described as an artist related to French Impressionism. At the same time, however, the whole development of his work was in step with the European Symbolist Movement. In the visual arts, he is one of its most important representatives. When Frink says, as she does here, that in her later work 'each piece is now a kind of vessel', she is consciously or unconsciously aligning herself with basic Symbolist doctrine. One reason for her artistic isolation in the later part of her career was that she was a belated product of Symbolism. Its ideas continue to form the theoretical underpinning of much contemporary art, but are now not often as directly expressed as they are in some of Frink's sculpture.

I like to work in good light – it's one reason why I enjoyed working in France. The change, going from London to the south, was enormous, because the light there was so clear and sharp. It affected my work in the sense that I went from doing very rough, textured sculptures in London to surfaces which were rather smooth and worked over – filed. I think this was entirely due to the change of light – it had begun to irritate me, having rough textures. I was irritated by the difference, by the shadows within the texture. But I've now gone through that phase, to rougher textures again.

At night I go to the studio when it's pitch black outside and switch the electric lights on. It throws all the texture into relief, every tiny mark on the surface. And that tells me a lot of things about what might be wrong with the sculpture I'm working on. Another reason for doing it is that I work in plaster, which is very white, and in daylight the surface is very flattened. Even on a grey day it's difficult for many people to understand what it might look like in bronze. I can do this, of course, but it's helpful to check. When looking at a piece of sculpture which is still in plaster, most spectators can't believe the kind of change that will happen when it's finally cast in bronze – the resonance given by a different colour.

I think my work is now more compact, with less obvious textures – it's become much more contained within the last four years, more intensified within itself, within each piece. What I'm trying to achieve in my figures and my heads is a sense of containment, of energy inside. The outward expression is

Leonardo's Dog II, bronze (1992) – inspired by a visit to Amboise, where Leonardo da Vinci spent his last years.

49

now less obvious than it was in my earlier work. Each piece is now a kind of vessel, and this means that the outward appearance can be much blander.

Nowadays the garden we have at Woolland, and the surrounding Dorset landscape, are important. I love the fact that we've got both trees and undulating ground. Most of the older pieces I have on the property stay where they are, but the rest move round pretty much like clockwork. We have great fun — we move the whole lot with a tractor. The tractor does for the farm, and it does for moving the sculptures too. For me the whole thing is very useful, because I see each piece in a different light. Even the silhouettes change; it's quite exhilarating. And I like arranging the sculptures in different groups, to see the relationships.

Frink was very much aware of the fact that her sculptural activity was in large part a search for archetypes, and it used to bother her slightly that her audience often did not see this as clearly as she saw it herself. Linked to this was a slightly different source of irritation — that many spectators were intent on ignoring the self-discipline which a working artist's life entailed.

The reason why I sculpt dogs and horses is nothing to do with whether it's a foxhound or a bulldog or whatever. It's just a *dog*, and dogs tend to bring certain ideas to my mind. My dogs are currently a little bit related to the Hungarian vizslas we have at Woolland, but that's because they're here. The particular attraction for me is that dogs are the animals who've been closest to man for thousands of years. I find that interesting.

In the same way the horse sculptures are nothing to do with the horses you see here in England — the hunter, the show horse, the race horse. They're much more to do with the ancient spirit of the horse and with its evolution in relation to man. For example, the fact that I was brought up with horses and taught to ride from an early age had no bearing on the horses I did in France. Those came about because I discovered the Camargue. I actually bought a horse, not having ridden myself for years — I bought one for my son to ride. So then I had a horse about. I used to go down to the Camargue and ride with the local cowboys.

Because you work on your own as an artist you have to be extremely disciplined — the public has a very strange idea of what artists are about. They

The garden at Woolland under snow, late 1980s.

50

think they are all bohemians like Augustus John – I suppose he was the last of them. That artists work when they like, play when they like, and that art is a wonderful hobby to have. People often say to me, 'I suppose you work when you feel like it.' Well, the answer is that once you're doing what you're doing you work very hard, and do it for most of your life.

Like nearly all contemporary artists – though unlike some of the great artists of the past, such as Rubens, who often seems to have worked more or less in public, while conversing with visitors and dictating letters to a secretary – Frink had a need for creative privacy. She did not at all mind explaining her creative processes, but being observed when she was actually at work was an entirely different matter. This need for privacy certainly played its part in her long-standing resistance to the idea of making use of assistants.

I don't like being watched working. When they made films of me at work I found the camera very intrusive. I find it an irritation to have anyone else in the studio because the way in which I work is very personal, putting on the plaster with my own hands, cutting it off, adjusting it. My real assistants are my bronze-casters. I can't do without them, and at least they're not working on top of me. Even then I like to have the last word. When the bronze comes back I work on it myself – I feel I must have the last touch on everything of mine that goes out of the studio. I think that's normal. Most artists prefer to do that.

I also don't like pieces going out too soon – I hate having to finish something against time, then having to hand it over immediately. I quite like to have slightly earlier pieces around when I'm working on something else.

In the end nothing is ever totally satisfactory. I feel very strongly that you can be pleased with a piece, that you're allowed to be pleased with a piece, but if you let yourself be totally satisfied you'll end up repeating yourself. You've got to go on. There are early pieces of mine which seem to me more important than others, and I'm bound to like those more. They're key pieces – usually something came from them. Looking back, I think I've developed quite slowly – my work falls into decades.

When I'm really into working it all happens somehow. I don't have to stop too much. Once I'm into a piece I just get on with it because I've already done my thinking – I've done that when I was setting the armature up. It's funny – I

Working on one of the *Desert Quartet* heads in front of the studio, 1989.

52

used to smoke, and the only time when I miss smoking now is in the studio. Because I'd stop, and have a look at what I'd done and have a fag. Never a whole one; usually just half of one. It's the only time I miss it.

Frink was aware of an apparent dichotomy in her work — that the traditionalism of her approach to materials and processes might seem to be in conflict with her claim to be a fully contemporary sculptor. She was always interested in younger artists who seemed, like herself, to be re-exploring traditional methods of making. This was one reason, though not the only one, why she was enthusiastic about the work of younger British sculptors such as Glynn Williams and Nicola Hicks, who seemed to be taking this direction.

In the last few years of her life she was increasingly fascinated by the whole question of new and different types of patination. Her late bronzes are often tinted in the boldest hues the processes of patination would give her. She liked to apply these patinas herself, and the chemicals she used were so toxic that one wonders if they had any connection with her fatal illness.

The materials you use for sculpture really depend on what you want the sculptures to do, and where you want them to be. Some materials just don't stand up to the weather. Bronze-casting is now so expensive that for a lot of young sculptors the cost is prohibitive, and that's why they have to use other materials. I think a lot of the really young ones are now turning to stone-carving. I carved quite a bit in stone myself, early on. I did nothing really memorable but I quite enjoyed it. I now keep on thinking that I must get a piece of stone and try again. The way I make my large heads, carving them out in plaster, might just as well be done in stone. I think it would be a nice thing to do — I love stone. Wood is far more difficult, because it has a fibre and it's quirky. If I went back to carving I'd prefer stone.

The idea of craftsmanship does interest me to a certain extent, but not overwhelmingly. I'm interested in the techniques of bronze-casting because I have such a lot to do with it. And what does interest me more and more is patination. I don't like other people to do it: I want to do it myself. I don't want to do brown bronzes any more, the way the Victorians did them. I want to use much more brilliant hues. And obviously that's much more difficult to sort out because you're still very limited in the colours you can get. I'm still trying to get

Working outdoors on one of the *Desert Quartet* heads, 1989.

54

this marvellous ultramarine I have in my mind. You can get blue-greens and green-blue or even turquoise, but not ultramarine. I want to make a completely blue person, using chemicals, not paint.

Right when I started off on this colour thing, I painted some bronzes, but it was hopeless. Paint doesn't weather well — it soon looks tacky. Another thing is that using paint means putting an extra skin on top of the surface, whereas the chemicals used for patination react directly on the surface you have.

We do all the patination here at Woolland. You've got to wear a mask because the materials are very toxic. You heat the bronze up with a gas torch, then, when it's really sizzling hot, you slosh on the chemicals till the bronze changes colour. It's magic. I'm not simply interested in blues. I'm also very interested now in using earth colours — red oxides.

In her studio at Woolland, with the plaster for *Man* (1982).

IV

Elisabeth Frink acknowledged – how could she fail to do so? – that she had over the years, though largely inadvertently, built up a certain position as a public figure. She was, however, always extremely wary of letting the 'public' aspect of her life get in the way of the private, creative one. It was for this reason – among others, such as her attachment to country life – that she so firmly turned aside the suggestion that she might become the first woman President of the Royal Academy.

It is a measure of how far matters have changed in the British art world, in the course of just over two centuries, that an artist mentioned as a possible PRA could also, and with some reason, speak of herself as an outsider. Curiously enough, the Tate Gallery's neglect of her work stung far less than what she perceived as the indifference, if not outright hostility, of the visual arts department of the British Council. The official acknowledgement she would have most liked eluded her – help in making her work better known abroad. She never made an explicit comparison – or not in my hearing – but she must certainly have contrasted this with the lavish help the Council gave to Henry Moore at a crucial point in his career.

I've been a trustee of the British Museum, a member of the Royal Fine Art Commission and I was very briefly a member of the committee which advises the Royal Mint. Sir Hugh Casson got me on to that, then I very quickly got myself off it. I must say now that when I look at our coins I'm upset about them. The only one which is at all nice is the pound.

The British Museum I enjoyed enormously, because being a trustee is all to do with lovely objects – things which had a lot to do with my own work. It was much broader than officiating on something which was to do with my immediate contemporaries, and that's why I stayed a long time – fifteen

In her studio at Woolland, 1981, with the *Walking Madonna* for Salisbury Cathedral Close.

Frink in the late 1960s.

Goggle Head II, bronze (1969). The *Goggle Heads* preoccupied Frink during her period in France. They were originally inspired by newspaper photographs.

years. I enjoyed every bit of it. The museum is an amazing place, and there were fascinating people among the other trustees. One or two were rather terrifying, like Dame Katherine Kenyon – a large, wide lady who was a bit like a walking primitive sculpture.

I didn't really enjoy the Royal Fine Art Commission. It was nice when you were dealing with nice people, but a lot of the stuff we were asked to look at was very mediocre. It was hard to find anything good in it.

Despite doing these jobs, however – it's difficult for me to say this – I do think that in contemporary art terms I'm an outsider. In particular, I've had an unsatisfactory relationship with the British Council. On the whole I never bothered about it, but it became irritating when important collectors used to ask me, 'Why weren't you represented in such-and-such a British exhibition abroad?' The only time I ever wrote to the Council asking for help was quite recently, when the Australians wanted to do an exhibition of my work. They wanted to show me as a senior artist, alongside someone who was conceptual, but didn't have the money to do it. So I wrote to the Council and got a very nice letter back saying that they couldn't support an exhibition of that kind. I have, nevertheless, managed to get by and get my work shown around the world.

I've had much more support from the Arts Council, who have contributed to the cost of various commissions.

Of course, while I say that I feel I'm an outsider, I also know that I'm recognised. I remember Leslie Waddington saying to me once, 'You should stop becoming a public figure and get on with it – do some work.' It wasn't entirely deserved because I was in fact working very hard. But in his opinion I was perhaps allowing my public image to interfere with my work. I don't think this was actually the case, but it was quite an interesting remark. It had something valid inside it.

The point is that if a large part of the public know your work – if you become visible to many people – then the critics just don't want to know. For some reason or other the situation irritates them. 'If you're a popular artist,' they say, 'what you make can't be good art.' Is it necessarily bad, or banal, because so many people like it?

60

Frink's career supplies proof, if any is needed, that it is perfectly possible to be a

highly successful, popular and well-established modern artist, while at the same time being almost entirely out-of-favour with most of the leading critics of the day. Artists' complaints about critics often sound like paranoia, but a search of the record proves that she was correct in claiming that there had been little critical writing of any interest which attempted to deal with her work.

I find that the critics have sometimes been helpful, but a lot of the time they've been amazingly destructive. I think all that has no point. If someone doesn't like your work, they have a perfect right to say so and give their reasons, but they shouldn't try to stop other people from looking. There's a kind of criticism which destroys an artist's work.

I've seen some pretty awful things written about my own work, where the tone has become personal – and that's upsetting. The trouble is that you do read them. You must say, 'Oh, I'm not going to read the bloody things. To hell with it, I don't give a damn!' But of course you do, and it's only human to feel hurt. But, having said that, I really don't get as upset as I used to.

As far as I can see there has been very little analytical criticism of my work, as opposed to the hurried stuff you get in newspapers. The only exceptions have been pieces written for exhibition catalogues. Either my work is so totally obvious that there's nothing to analyse – and that's a possibility – or I'm not the right flavour.

During the time that I've been working – forty years now – there have been enormous changes in art. In the way of doing it, the way of looking at it, the way of dealing with the public – the whole scene has changed. There are more places to see art than there ever have been before. The most dramatic changes have been in sculpture, even though many of the so-called innovations turn out to be things which have been done before, by people like Marcel Duchamp and the Constructivists.

In my view critics haven't understood the historical and intellectual background to my work. I can remember William Feaver, for example, dismissing my *Goggle Heads* when they were included in a Hayward Annual. He disposed of them very summarily as 'stupid, boring *Goggle Heads*'. I was cross about that, because they meant something to me, something quite important. And after all, they are likenesses of stupid people – portraits of stupidity, cruelty and

Easter Head, bronze (1989). This shows Frink's use of differential patination. The word 'Easter' refers not to Easter Island but to the Resurrection.

63

inhumanity. Brainless, nasty people. A statement on my part about the cruelty and stupidity of repressive régimes, and of the men who operated them. I also remember Marina Vaizey denouncing the banality of my work 'which the English public has taken to its collective breast'. She was most aggressive. She seemed to take it personally that a lot of the public like my work – she implied that they were idiots too. I find that senseless.

However, having complained that critics are too personal, I also don't think my work responds very well to formalist criticism – criticism through form. I get irritated by it, because I'm not quite sure what I'm doing anyway.

What I think I'm doing is creating my own myths – I'm not the slightest bit interested in other people's myths. To look at, yes, but not as sources for my own work. For example, I'm not interested in the Greek myths. I don't want to use them as an inspiration for what I do – I make images of flight, but they're nothing to do with Icarus. I'm not like Michael Ayrton, who was definitely a Greek-myth man. It's too literary. None of my things is to do with ancient myths, with the possible exception of the *Green Man*. I just work out of my head.

My series are my narratives, but I'm not intellectual at all in my approach to my work. It's a question of finding an image which is psychologically right for me. All my images are something that's happened to me first – I'm very bad at putting what I want to say into words. I think that what I'm doing is trying to set up a kind of encounter with the spectator, a dialogue between my sculptures and the public. People have to add part of themselves to make it work; they have to look into it as well as at it.

The most helpful kind of criticism would be something which helped people to understand the various ideas which might have gone through my – the artist's – head, at the time when I was making it. It does bother me if people come up with explanations which are so far off beam that they become ridiculous. The *Easter Heads*, for instance, are about Easter and the Resurrection, but nothing to do with Easter Island. On the whole, however, it's really up to the viewers to make what they like out of what I do.

There is a certain injustice in Frink's claim, below, that only Bryan Robertson and I discussed her sculpture seriously with her. Sarah Kent's excellent introductory essay for Frink's 1985 retrospective at the Royal Academy of Arts in London must surely have been based on in-depth conversations with the artist. It was unusual for Frink to make a slip of this kind; she was always anxious to give their full due, and perhaps more than their due, to any collaborators she might have worked with.

The reason, in this case, may have been uneasiness concerning Sarah Kent's firmly feminist stance. The discourse which follows covers a number of topics, but its chief value is that it throws a great deal of light on Frink's feelings about her own situation as a woman who made art. She always denied — it was the cornerstone of her position in the matter — having met with any real prejudice because of her gender. This denial made some embattled feminists feel that she was a traitor to the cause. On the other hand, the account she gives of her exhibition at the Women's Museum in Washington shows that she was aware of some of the pitfalls which lay in wait for women as they tried to assume a more prominent role in the world of contemporary art.

However, her vivid description of her meeting with Barbara Hepworth implies that she also saw the situation in a much broader context — for her the battle between the

With a group of *Goggle* and *Tribute* heads, late 1970s.

65

generations was at least as important as the battle between the sexes. Critics and curators were involved in both of these – seldom to the benefit of artists.

Bryan Robertson and you are about the only art critics I've talked to seriously. Way back in the 1960s I remember talking to Terence Mullaly, who was then writing for the *Telegraph*, and also, in New York, to Hilton Kramer. When I was in New York I also talked to Clement Greenberg, but not specifically about what I was doing as an artist. I think critics on either side of the Atlantic have tended to make much the same points about my work.

For me, there are two categories of critics – the serious critics of the day, who do only art criticism, and journalists. I find that a lot of newspapers seem to switch their critics around, so you find somebody doing art criticism, then they pop up doing something else. I just don't understand this – one wonders what the qualifications are. My feeling is that art critics ought to have a good grounding in art history. They should be to some extent art historians, and know what they are talking about. Lots of artists do use the past as a context for what they are creating in the present, and the critic must have some knowledge of what they are doing.

Having said this, I myself am probably one of the few artists whose knowledge of the history of art is sadly defective. In the broad sense I know very little of art history and art-historical periods. While I enjoyed doing history at school, I've forgotten most of it. The reason may be that I'm concentrating on my own creative realm, and just go and look at the parts of history and periods of art that happen to appeal to me. For the artist, it isn't the structure of movements and that kind of thing which matters, but the one little aspect which is actually important to him personally.

Curators are almost more of a problem than critics. Today you are sadly at a disadvantage as an artist if you are not beloved by the curators of your time. I'm not anti-museums of modern art, because they are an essential part of our culture. But all museum collections are shaped by curators whose views are very much personal ones.

My exhibition in Washington at the Women's Museum there [1991] was an interesting experience because one was aware of the fact that the museum was very much looked down on by all the other museum people – the directors of

In France, early 1970s.

Above: Head of the full-length portrait of Elisabeth Frink by F. E. McWilliam (*c*. 1950).

Above left: On the Dorset downs, late 1970s or early 1980s.

Left: The studio at Woolland, with the *Horse* for Goodwood still in plaster, 1980.

Above: Working on *Seated Man*, *c.* 1983. Friends sometimes remarked on its resemblance to her husband, Alex Csáky.

Left: In the studio with one of the figures from the *Dorset Martyrs* group, plus *Standing Man*, *c.* 1982–3.

Opposite: In the studio with the unfinished plaster of one of the Hong Kong *Water-buffaloes*, 1987.

Above: The studio at Woolland with *Running Man* in plaster, *c.* 1985–6.

Above right: With two heads from *Desert Quartet* (now in bronze, but patinated white), *c.* 1990.

Right: The north front, Woolland House. Originally a large stable-block, the buildings were later converted into a residence.

Top: Frink's fancy chickens — the subject of her correspondence with the Duchess of Devonshire.

Bottom: The large dining hall at Woolland.

Above: Frink did not usually do portraits of females, but made an exception in the case of herself, when asked to participate in the touring exhibition *The Self Portrait: A Modern View*. The result — an extremely good likeness — was made at the height of her fascination with colour, and makes effective use of her mass of curly white hair.

Right: *Birdman*, drawing (*c*. 1950).

Above: *Judas*, bronze (1963). Frink considered this to be a key piece in her development.

Above left: *Dying King*, bronze (1963) – partly inspired by the closing scene of Sir Laurence Olivier's film of Shakespeare's *Richard III*.

Left: *Wild Boar*, bronze (1975) – inspired by those seen in the Cevennes, but made later.

Right: *Stretching Figure*, watercolour (1967).

Opposite: *General Oufkir*, watercolour (1966).
The dark glasses always worn by the
Algerian politician General Oufkir were a
source of inspiration for the *Goggle Heads*.

Fiink 66

Above: *Mirage I* and *Mirage II*, aluminium (1967 and 1969). The forms were suggested by some of the strange optical effects typical of the Camargue.

Above right: *Three Mirages*, bronze (1967) — studies for the larger sculptures of the same title. These are among Frink's more abstract works.

Right: *Barking Dog*, bronze (1981) — based on one of the Hungarian vizslas Elisabeth Frink and Alex Csáky kept at Woolland, but not, as she pointed out, an exact portrait of the breed.

Above: *Running Man*, bronze (1978).

Left: *Running Man*, bronze (1978).

Above: *Walking Madonna* for Salisbury Cathedral Close, bronze (1981). This is one of Frink's very rare female figures. She complained that she had trouble with the drapery.

Right: *Flying Men*, bronze (1982).

Above: *Horse*, bronze (1980).

Left: *War Horse*, bronze (1991). The sculpture is shown in position at Chatsworth.

Above: *Riace I*, bronze (1986).

Right: Portrait of Lin Jammet, bronze (1980). A little over a decade later, Frink was to take some hints for her *Risen Christ* from her son's appearance.

Above: *Horsehead I*, drawing in acrylic and charcoal on paper (1988). During the last years of her career Frink made a series of brilliantly-coloured drawings, inspired in part by a trip to Australia. The use of streaks of red suggests that the horse is wounded. The drawing is related to *War Horse* (1991).

Left: *Man with Baboon*, acrylic and charcoal on paper (1990) – one of a series of large-scale drawings on this theme. Frink also wanted to make a sculptural group of the same subject.

Green Man, bronze (1991). The sculpture
was inspired by William Anderson's book
Green Man, which Frink was given when
recuperating from her first bout of cancer.

67

the National Gallery and the Hirschhorn. They viewed the whole thing with such suspicion. One already felt at a disadvantage, having an exhibition there, as though it was really *infra dig*.

I remember that, just before the opening, the Women's Museum gave a lunch for local critics and journalists. I sat next to a young critic who later gave me a hostile review – the only bad review, I think. And he was so arrogant and distant. He appeared to find it demeaning that it was a female institution – which really made me very angry. I find it rather sad that it's necessary to have a special Women's Museum at all. I don't think women should have to make a point by having their own galleries, their own exhibitions. To my mind if you're an artist, it doesn't matter if you're masculine or feminine. You either create a good image or a bad one.

If I felt prejudice in Washington it was from critics and curators, not from any of the gallery-goers. I like the American public. I admire their enthusiasm for going to exhibitions. In Washington, hundreds of people came. In fact, it was very interesting, because finally, and rather grudgingly, the museum people came and saw it. I was told that it was the first time that many of them had ever set foot in the place. The curators from the other museums in Washington had never actually been near it. So one felt prejudice there. Yet I must say that the team of young women who ran the place were brilliant, and my show was beautifully arranged. You couldn't have had better conditions for viewing my work. I was interested by what many of the women artists I met in America said to me – always the same thing – that they felt they would never be given the opportunity to have a show in a museum: it just wasn't on.

I never felt prejudice as a woman artist in this country. Yet, having said that, I do feel that it's been difficult for a woman to have a museum show here. Barbara Hepworth had a museum show, but I've never been offered one. The Tate wouldn't touch me. In the end I had a show at the Royal Academy, which was marvellous, because it is so accessible. If I were to have another one now in London, I'd still want one there. I'd choose the RA's Sackler Galleries, because they're so beautiful architecturally. But there is a kind of museum preconception against me even here.

Changes in fashion can be very hard even on a well-established artist. I once had a very interesting conversation with Barbara, actually at the Tate. There

In her studio working on *First Man*, 1964.

68

was a big exhibition of British art — 1960 or 1961 was it? And they had included my piece *First Man*. I was excited to show there, because I was still quite young. And even more excited and honoured to find myself talking to Hepworth, because she always seemed a tiny bit frightening to me. On that particular day she really seemed to want to talk; she was obviously quite pleased when I introduced myself to her. We hadn't been introduced before.

It soon became clear that she was really worried about her work at that precise moment. I couldn't understand it then, but I suddenly realised now that here she was, in an exhibition filled with the work of an enormous number of young people, and she was apprehensive because of that. It's only now, in my old age so to speak, that I suddenly find myself thinking, 'My God, one's sixty, and here are all these exciting new sculptors coming on.' You do feel a bit apprehensive in a way, as if you ought perhaps to make an effort to do something. To do more. But what? You ask yourself, 'Have I done enough?' It's only now that I understand Barbara's attitudes. At the time I was just amazed that she should be so worried, so fussed. I never met her again. She had an extraordinary face. I remember Tony Snowdon's photograph of her — on the rocks, down in Cornwall. It was not long after that that his book came out: *Private View.*

Thinking about that meeting reminds me that the early 1960s were a good time for me. But to go back to the question of prejudice against women. I never felt prejudice during that time here in England, or at any other time. But I've often felt that the museums were definitely against me. Not because of my gender, but because I'm a figurative sculptor. They're not prejudiced against abstract sculptors. And things are changing. If you look at the Turner Prize short lists, there are quite a few women on them now.

Frink was not by instinct political — the fervid political engagement typical of so much twentieth-century art was alien to her. Nevertheless, the generosity of her instincts led her to react strongly against certain political events; these feelings do inevitably colour her work, though the allusions she makes are seldom specific. She took part in the competition for a monument to the Unknown Political Prisoner, and her engagement with the theme was far from factitious: she was a supporter of Amnesty International throughout her career — often, as she notes, in the face of

First Man, bronze (1962).

opposition from politically conservative friends. In her earlier years, it was events abroad which tended to catch her attention — for example, the reaction, both in France and in Algeria, to the aftermath of the Algerian War of Independence. It was only in the 1980s that the actions of the Thatcher government focused her attention on what was taking place at home. Despite her undoubted indignation, her opposition to what was happening in Britain found little or no direct expression in her sculpture.

The only thing I really support formally is Amnesty International — Amnesty is my main thing, and I've done posters for them. Obviously I can't give them large sums of money myself, but my work has raised quite a lot for them. It's not always a popular commitment. People say, 'How can you support that? It's Communist.' They have this obsession about Amnesty being totally left wing. Of course Amnesty supports people who've suffered under left-wing régimes as well as under right-wing ones.

Even though I've never had any party politics, I do mind about what happens in this country. As I've got older I've become more critically conscious of our own government. I mind the injustices very much. I was very anti-Thatcher because I felt it was a time of philistinism, a time of greed. Mind you, that also applied to the art world, the art market. The only thing that mattered was what was happening at the top of the tree — everything else got forgotten. People just forgot a whole section of the community.

My concerns as an artist are humanitarian, not really political. Images with apparent political echoes are just comments — comments about inhumanity.

Her religious attitudes were in some ways very like those of other members of her generation and class. She felt alienated from all forms of organised religion, and perhaps most of all from the faith in which she had been brought up, that of the Catholic Church. Her disillusionment with Catholicism was based on what she saw as the stupidity and even wickedness of its social policies, especially in the Third World. She also, like many Catholics, deplored the fact that the mass was now said in the vernacular. For her, this robbed it of nearly all its sacred aura.

Despite this alienation, however, she continued to think of herself as a believer. She enjoyed working on church commissions, and the religious images she created were never cynical or opportunistic. There is within them the force of genuine belief.

Working on her *Midas*, 1989. In the foreground is one of the heads from *Desert Quartet*.

73

I don't think I was ever particularly religious. I just took it for granted that I would be brought up as a Catholic like my mother, because my mother in turn had been brought up in the religion of her mother, who was an Irishwoman, while her brother took after his father, who was a Scottish Presbyterian. My brother and I were brought up as Catholics: Daddy was Church of England. I was brought up and educated in convents, mostly by French nuns, and of course the mass was very enjoyable to go to. The early chants – we always had beautiful sung mass where I was.

I haven't really remained in touch with the Church. I disagree with so many of the things they've done or are failing to do all over the world at the moment, and I think the present Pope has been terribly unconstructive. If you've been to Mexico City you understand the poverty there, but when the Pope goes there he pats them on the head and congratulates them on their large families. And they're all dying of disease or starvation. This is happening all over the world where the Catholic Church exercises a major influence.

Another reason I've dropped out of touch is the fact that they've changed the mass. They thought they could better it, and so they rewrote it. They decided the Latin was difficult, whereas it was Latin which made the mass the same all over the world, so that wherever you went to church, you could understand it. To ruin such beautiful words and meanings and turn them into banality! I can't listen to it in English.

Yet I am a Christian. I feel Christian, and I think that being Christian is a matter of believing in another power, believing in God. I believe in the survival of the spirit, and of the soul. The spirit of people lives on, and is always there. I am not sure that I believe in an afterlife in my present form, or my present body, but I would hope that my spirit in another form would continue to be there.

Frink's empathy with Christian doctrine could be seen as forming part of a powerful imaginative life. She was a great reader – Woolland was always full of books. Significantly, she preferred fiction to biography or art history, and among fiction writers her choice often fell on the great Latin American novelists of the present century – the so-called Magical Realists – and upon other novelists who resembled them, such as the German writer Günter Grass, whose extraordinary book The Tin Drum *she particularly relished.*

Working on the *Midas* head.

76

I read a lot, because I enjoy reading very much. I read something every day, usually late at night or early in the morning, because I don't sleep very well. When I was at school I read romantic novels – *The Scarlet Pimpernel* and all that stuff. Later I got to like Dickens and Shakespeare. When I was a young woman I read Evelyn Waugh and Aldous Huxley – *Brave New World*. And I liked the poems of Rilke. In the 1960s I read William Faulkner from beginning to end. I sometimes get hooked on a writer and read everything he's written. I've read all the books of the Australian writer Patrick White – *Riders in the Chariot* and so forth.

Currently the sort of books I like are novels by Iris Murdoch and Gabriel García Márquez. I tend to like the leading Latin American writers very much – Castaneda, Carlos Fuentes, Mario Vargas Llosa. I don't know why I like them so much – they're totally different from my own culture. I'm also very hooked on Günter Grass, though the atmosphere of his books is much more northern. Among younger writers there's Marina Warner; I've just read a book of hers called *Indigo*, which I liked very much.

The novels I read are usually books with a strong imaginative content, and I think the work of many of the writers I've named runs very much parallel with my own work as an artist. As I've said before, I live very much in my mind. I'm much more interested in fantasy, in something really strange, than I am in biography, though right at the moment I'm reading a life of the explorer Richard Burton. I hardly ever read art history, though books about archaeology sometimes interest me. For instance I recently read a book about early Celtic art.

Granted this relish for modern literature, it was not surprising that Frink and her husband Alex Csáky tended to find the art world socially rather confining. In any case, Frink seems to have followed a pattern not entirely uncommon among successful artists – and also, for that matter, among successful writers. In their younger days, they live very intensely in the company of a peer group which is interested in the same art form. As their work matures, they move out of this narrow circle, and often find that people who practise other disciplines have more to tell them.

With her third husband, Alex Csáky, late 1970s.

A lot of artists don't really talk to each other. I haven't talked to other artists much since the 1950s, when I used to talk to Kenneth Armitage, Lynn

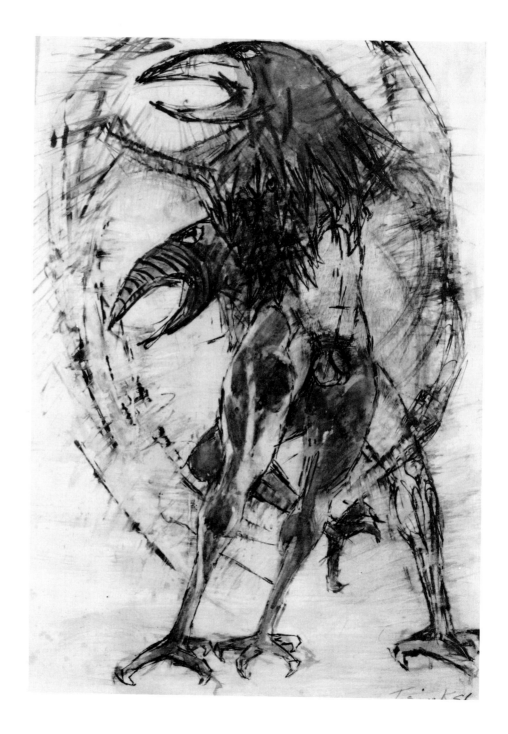

78

Chadwick, Bernard Meadows because he taught me, Caro in the early days before he changed direction. Then in the 1960s I moved out of London. I've always been a countrywoman by temperament, even in the days when I still lived in London. When I picked myself up and went to live in a very remote part of France, my life took on a very different pattern. I like what cities have to offer – going to the theatre, the opera and so forth, and I go when I can, but I'm perfectly happy to live here in Dorset. I'd hate to have to work in a city – I have to work here. And while I like meeting artists very much, I really do, I long ago realised that a lot of them don't really want to have discussions about art.

I'm perfectly happy to talk to people who do quite different things from what I do. When we lived in France I knew Larry Durrell very well. He was totally eccentric, very up and down. I was very fond of him, but he could be wicked – very wicked about other people. His writing by that time was very strange: I liked his late books but most people didn't. Perhaps it was because I knew the background to them. Our final exchange of letters was very funny. He'd got to know a Buddhist commune, and he wanted me to sculpt a life-size elephant for them which in some way or other was going to make them a lot of money.

Today, while our main friends have certainly come to us through my work, we actually see a very wide spectrum – country people, doctors, senior actors, a lot of musicians, a few good friends who are architects. I get a lot of stimulus from them – I'm fairly gregarious, but not much of a person for artistic groups.

One thing which Frink stressed constantly in conversation, both on and off the record, was her love of music. Music and musical forms seemed to have some intimate relationship to her creative process which she couldn't completely articulate. This is a subject I would like to have pursued further – the discussion was cut short by Frink's death.

Music has been important to me ever since I was a child. My father liked music and I really wanted to learn the piano. I used to mess around on it, but we couldn't afford for me to take two extra classes. We were very hard up and I already did art. I still wish I could play the piano because it's a most beautiful,

Two Birds, drawing (1956).

80

Moving sculptures at Woolland, *c.* 1983.

intimate instrument. I'd like to be able to play just for myself, to sit down and play. I love it when friends come here and play. My good friend John Drummond is a brilliant pianist.

I like to have music while I'm working. I prefer chamber music to concertos and symphonies – virtuoso quartets and quintets. And I like to know what's going on in music now: John Tavener, Harrison Birtwistle, things like that. I also respond very much to opera. I like Janáček, and I'm beginning to like Wagner. I never used to like him, but we recently bought a lot of Wagner recordings and I'm starting to get into them. I'd quite like to design an opera. People at Covent Garden were always saying to me, 'I say, I say, I say, would you like to design an opera?' 'Yes,' I'd say, but nothing ever came of it. It's a closed shop.

In the studio what I listen to is rather dictated by Radio 3. There's so much plaster and plaster dust around, any CD-player or tape-recorder suffers. I'm

Birdman, bronze (1959) – a classic image from the earlier part of Frink's career.

disgusted that they've gone back to cutting out music on Radio 3 and putting on the bloody test match.

Indicative of Frink's strong imaginative life were her dreams. Though she claimed she never actually used a dream to work from, the connection between the dream imagery she described and her repertoire of sculptural images is clear.

I do dream, and I used to dream a lot more. But I do still have bouts of dreaming. I have very strange dreams of flight, dreams of birds and dreams involving animals – rather allegorical. I don't know if they feed into my work. I don't think I've ever actually used a dream to work from.

I generally remember my dreams to a certain extent, when they're very special and have strong images. I had one the other day in which I was standing somewhere and huge bird shapes would roar past, soar up beside me till the sky was full of them. Someone said it was because I keep chickens – because of my obsession with chickens. In fact I've had this flight dream from the time I was very young. It's to do with birds flying, planes crashing – big monstrous things

With a portrait bust of her by Robert Clatworthy, 1984. Frink and Clatworthy were fellow students at Chelsea.

83

flying, sometimes with a man in them. I don't have many dreams about horses. I dream of dogs sometimes, but not horses.

Frink never pretended that making art wasn't a business. Throughout the latter part of her career she acted as her own dealer, selling work direct from Woolland and also arranging gallery shows on an ad hoc basis. She was fortunate because the commercial aspect of her career wasn't in fact a burden to her: she ran it with the same brisk practicality which she brought to managing the household at Woolland.

The rise in prices for contemporary art is probably on balance a very good change. I don't think it should be absolutely necessary for the artist to grub along. It's a depressing doctrine that seriously good art comes from being seriously poor.

Being a sculptor is inherently much more expensive than being a painter. Because of casting costs, the outlay is enormous. I suppose you make up for it in the end by being able to do editions. But it doesn't matter whether you're a painter or a sculptor: you've still got to pay the rent.

In the early days my dealer, the Waddington Gallery, helped with casting costs. It's a very good system for young artists starting out if they can either be helped out with their materials or else be put on some kind of retainer. In my case I was very lucky, because I started selling work reasonably early.

Now I deal for myself – I'm a totally free enterprise. And that raises its own problems. We have to have a secretary and a fax machine. The house and garden are my gallery, so people come here. You have to be careful to keep working and dealing separate; not to let one get in the way of the other. And there are other problems too, which a dealer would normally take care of. I have to send stuff all over the world, and it's expensive.

One thing you run into when you've been established for a long time is the whole question of the secondary market. Things come up in the auction rooms, and you hope they're going to make a decent price. Some of them may be things you no longer have yourself. On the whole I don't go into the market in order to buy things back. I've only done it once or twice, because I really wanted something.

Running Man, bronze (1980).

85

86

Nowadays I try to keep an example of everything I make. At the beginning, I didn't do that – unlike Henry Moore, who did it all his life. But I do now have a representative collection. One reason I've been able to put this together is the retrospective exhibition I had at the Royal Academy. I was able to borrow a lot of pieces back from collectors. Many of these were very helpful when I told them that I'd never in fact made my own artist's copy of whatever it was. They said, yes, I could have a cast made, and that's how I managed to get a collection together. Most of my editions are cast, and the casts are sold out.

What I've got in my own hands is a cross-section which gives a good idea of the various periods I've been through. I like to have them for their own sake – I look at the older pieces with interest. But I don't directly refer to them in new work; I remain very much outside them. Someone came up to me the other day and said would I consider doing another sculpture of a wild boar; and I said, 'Not really, because it's not something in the present.' In the same way I'll never do my birds again. It would be like going backwards.

At the same time, she took a rather cool view of the reactions of the British public to art. She was not an élitist, but she entertained no very high hope of a revolution in public attitudes.

The public have very odd ideas about artists. Most of them think you shouldn't have to pay more than thirty quid for a painting. Their feeling is that, since artists don't really work, why should art cost so much money? For the man in the street, an artist is a person who doesn't have a proper routine. But artists probably work longer hours than the person who is complaining. In fact the British are very undiscriminating visually, and the attitude to artists remains pretty primitive.

Perhaps it was because she was in fact an unusually generous contributor, both in cash and in kind, to the various good causes to which she gave her support, that Frink increasingly resented what she considered the unreasonable and insensitive demands of charity organisers.

In the garden at Woolland House, with one of the *Mirages*, c. 1991.

Nowadays some of the main pressures on successful artists are demands from charity auctions. An artist is supposed to hand over a painting which is worth perhaps two or three thousand quid, while the ordinary person will contribute perhaps a fiver to the same cause. But charity organisers won't see that this is inequitable. As a result a lot of artists are not helping charities any more. What I do personally is to support as many as I think I can. Then at some point in each year I come to the end of it, reach saturation point.

The final reply in this section was prompted by a question about the contents of Woolland House, which was furnished with an attractive and extremely personal mixture of furniture and objects. Especially prominent were bold, sculptural chairs, always with a quirky individuality of form; and Australian Aboriginal wood-carvings which mingled with Frink's own sculptures. As with many artists' houses, the interior was in its own way a self-portrait.

I've never been a great collector of art, though I have done swaps in the past with contemporaries. Now I wish I'd bought more, since everything has become so very expensive. For example, I wish I'd bought Craigie Aitchison a while ago. The modern British things I have are mostly friends' work, though I do have an Alfred Wallis from way back. More recently I've bought Australian Aboriginal work and things like that.

I do like creating an interesting space to live in – that's very important to me. I buy primitive furniture – old chairs and tables and cupboards – and I do look at them. I think they tie in very much with doing sculpture. I'd never live with Chippendale or ornate things of that sort.

One reason for not collecting a great deal of art by my contemporaries has always been space. You have to have enough room to put your own work up on the wall, and until we moved to Dorset I never really had a tremendous amount of wall space. And there's the problem of money. That's always the way, isn't it? When you do have some space, you don't have the money.

In any case, perhaps I've really been too keen on possessions recently. I was trying to sort things out in my mind the other day: 'If we lost all this, or had to move and sell off a tremendous amount of the stuff we have, would I really mind?' And I decided that no, I wouldn't. I think it's something to do with having had cancer. In fact, I'm sure it's to do with that. I now think it's necessary for us to change our lives in some way – to simplify, to become less orientated towards social gatherings and collecting this or collecting that. Those things don't really matter. In fact, they don't matter a damn. The only thing now is that I wouldn't throw all our stuff away, or even sell it. I might put it in a warehouse because I'd like my son to have it. Then he could do what he liked with it.

V

Many artists, as they mature, increasingly turn away from the work of their contemporaries. This was not true of Elisabeth Frink. Despite living in comparative isolation in the depths of the Dorset countryside, she continued to take a lively interest in the work of other artists, and particularly in that of sculptors younger than herself. One of the main purposes of her visits to London was to keep a finger on the pulse of what was going on in the art world.

My main way of finding out what is going on in art is to go to exhibitions. It's very difficult for artists not to lose their nerve. Things are changing all the time. There are new art movements, lots of new young talents coming up. However set you are in what you do, it can be quite disturbing. I felt quite shaken in the late 1960s and early 1970s, when everything seemed to be abstract and conceptual – was I actually being left behind? But you don't stick your head in the sand in those circumstances. You've got to be aware. Nowadays I make a point of looking at the work of younger sculptors whenever I can, though I haven't been able to do that as much as I'd like during the past two years because of my illness. I go along to the diploma shows at the Royal College of Art and at some of the other London colleges because I think that's one of the best ways of finding interesting things to look at. I think Glynn Williams was an excellent choice for Professor of Sculpture at the Royal College. His own work has always been very strong. For a long time the Royal College sculpture school had rather an unbalanced character. It seemed to be completely given over to environmental and conceptual work.

For me, Nicola Hicks is one of our most talented young sculptors, and also a most wonderful draughtsman. I think she's got it in her, and that she'll

With two *Desert Quartet* heads still in plaster, 1989.

Running Man II, bronze (1979).

probably be a very great artist one day. I've always followed her work, because I've known her since she was a child. I remember going to see her degree show, and thinking, 'This girl just shines out.'

There are suddenly a lot of tremendously strong figurative artists now, young artists working with the figure. It would take a huge amount of effort to push them all off course. But I think that, yes, there was a moment when I did have doubts. I always have doubts about my work. Questions about 'Why?' — 'What for?' Yet in the end I always knew that there was nothing in entirely abstract art for me, nothing which would fit in with my feelings about sculpture. The nearest I got to making fully abstract shapes were some pieces done in the early 1960s based on animal heads. That was my most abstract period. And even then I always felt you needed to use human or animal forms. I think you reach a moment with abstraction when it becomes a complete desert. It's very difficult to continue working in a totally abstract vein without any root in the visible. For me it wasn't available as an option, or I didn't want to avail myself of it. Yet of course I was worried, because there was a time when abstract work was so popular, and figurative work so unpopular.

However, throughout my career I've been on the buying, collecting side of the divide in the art world, not the intellectually fashionable side, and that's given me a lot of stability in many ways.

Frink was not naturally introspective about her own development. She was generally much more interested in what was going on in the external world than in contemplating possible sources for her own work. The answer given here, pieced together from replies to a number of different questions, may give a false impression, in that Frink was generally much less fluent than the flow of this now implies, when trying to sum up her own influences and possible source material. Like many twentieth-century Modernist sculptors she was strongly affected by primitive and ancient art. Here, once again, one seems to see the impact of Malraux's musée imaginaire.

I've been trying to trace my ideas back to why I did certain forms. One thing I know influenced me was aspects of Rodin — the way he translated anatomy into movement — into moving sinew and muscle. When I was young that was the thing I most wanted to emulate — especially his small, leaping figures. There's a real dynamic force in them. And I also very much liked Giacometti. Not so

92

much the actual formula, but the way he built up his work. And I also liked his attenuated legs. I did them for a long time myself.

Other influences have been sculptures from early civilisations. I like early Greek art, most of all the big *kouros* figures. I like Archaic Greek art, not the late stuff. And I've always liked pre-Columbian art – Mayan and Aztec – because I think it's very powerful. The head comes into it again. There's a lot of emphasis on the head in many of the pieces.

Medieval sculpture I like because I'm Nordic. Despite the time I spent in France I'm a northern person rather than a southern person. In East Anglia, where I was brought up, it's very bleak, very cold in winter. I still look at medieval sculpture whenever I can – for example, driving through France and Italy. I never make notes when I'm away, but I like to look.

I once made a sculpture – it's destroyed now – which was influenced by medieval work, and also perhaps by Manzù. I met him in London, and of course I saw some of his cardinals. It showed a full-length figure of a dead pope, laid out in state. But it was also influenced, just as much, by a photograph I saw of a dead pope lying in state – I think it may have been Pius XII. He had a rather extraordinary skull-like head and a beaky nose. It was an example, like the *Goggle Heads*, of the way photographs have been important to me as sources of ideas.

Yet I do think my ideas come mostly from inside myself. When I was a young artist I lived very much in my imagination, in my mind, and I think that was the real reason for a lot of the work I did. It didn't particularly come from anywhere. But people tend to leap to conclusions. When I started doing horses and horsemen, quite late in my career, people automatically assumed I was influenced by Marino Marini. And this wasn't the case at all. I actually find Marini's horsemen rather stark. They look as though they've been struck by lightning. I think my own horsemen go much further, to something more primitive than Marini. Uccello, perhaps. The reason why I sculpt horses is that they've been part of man's life for so many thousands of years. The sculptures by Marini that I do admire are his portraits, which are absolutely astonishing. I didn't know about them till quite recently, when I saw a book of portraits he'd done.

Frink often acknowledged a debt to Rodin. It is interesting to be reminded that he, who now seems, in terms of the Modern movement considered as a whole, a relatively

94

peripheral figure, was, in the early 1950s, still a sculptor of immediate interest to the artists of Frink's generation. It is almost equally interesting to be reminded that Epstein — now rather neglected — remained a towering figure in British art during that period. His reputation declined abruptly with the sudden change of artistic climate at the beginning of the 1960s.

I was immensely struck by Rodin. He was the first sculptor I discovered when I was a teenager — someone gave me a book about him. To me it seemed quite extraordinary what he did. Going to the Musée Rodin was the highlight of my first trip to Paris in 1951, when I was twenty-one. We walked everywhere and visited artists' studios. We saw Giacometti, but didn't talk to him. We used to hang out in Montparnasse, up by the Dôme, and we'd sit and watch him there. I thought he had a marvellous face. I wish I'd met him properly. I wouldn't have thought of approaching anyone like that — not when I was that age.

I knew Epstein quite well. I got to know him through the writer Laurie Lee, who married his niece. Epstein actually came to my first wedding, when I married Michel Jammet, and I often used to go to musical evenings at his house. However, I don't think he ever had any special effect on my sculpture, except for the fact that he was an example: he was really responsible for putting sculpture in front of the British public. His sources were different from anything else which had been known here, because he trained in Paris.

The interesting thing about Epstein, for me, is that the carvings are so different from the bronzes. When I was young I liked the bronzes, and now I think I like the carvings much more — certainly better than the late figures in bronze, which get out of hand: they're too rhetorical. I also think that his portraits of men are much better, less stereotyped, than his portraits of women.

The link between Frink's early work and that of Giacometti is a very logical one, given the artistic climate of the time, as is that between Frink and Germaine Richier. The fact that these links have been little discussed is perhaps due to the general tendency to neglect French art of the post-Second World War epoch. Giacometti, it is true, retains unique prestige, of a sort now denied to nearly all of his Paris contemporaries, but the tendency has been to stress precisely the quality of introversion which Frink singles out as marking his essential temperamental difference from herself.

Eagle Lectern for Coventry Cathedral, plaster for bronze (1962) — commissioned by the architect of the rebuilt cathedral, Sir Basil Spence, and one of several items Frink made for the building.

95

The bond between Frink and Paolozzi was clearly much more one of personal sympathy than of style. Her remark that Paolozzi's early work resembled that which Anthony Caro was doing at the same period throws an unexpected light on both sculptors.

At one time I felt artistically close to Giacometti. I don't quite know why, because our work is very unalike. In my early work I was, however, influenced by the way he built things up in plaster. But not by his actual approach. What he was doing was very different from what I was doing. He was much more cerebral — very enclosed and introverted. Germaine Richier did influence me when I was young. I met her once when she came to London. I thought she was a marvellous woman, very sympathetic.

I don't think I was influenced by Henry Moore, though he was always very nice to me and we got on well together. When I was a student at Chelsea he still used to come there from time to time and look at what we were doing. He was always very encouraging.

Paolozzi I've always admired, but not every period of his work. I don't like all that immensely complicated machinery stuff he once did, and all those equally complicated prints. I think things should be more earthy. But I did like the

New Bird II, bronze (1965).

With a mixed group of heads of different periods, Woolland, *c.* 1991.

97

In the studio with Anthony Sampson, who presented the television series *The Midas Touch*, and her stepson Mick Csáky, who directed it.

Horse for Goodwood, bronze (1980) – commissioned by the Earl of March. Frink noted that this was not meant to be an exact likeness of a thoroughbred, but an *idea* of a racehorse.

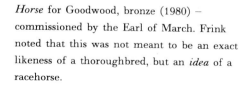

98

early things, and I like what he's doing now, when he's become more figurative. His recent self-portrait is amusing.

When I was young we were all very impressed by him. I remember that we met in a very funny way. Someone brought me a sculpture of a bull which was broken and asked if I could mend it. 'Whose sculpture is it?' – 'It's by a man called Paolozzi.' – 'Why don't you get him to do it?' – 'I don't know how to find him.' 'Well,' I said, 'I'm sure I do.' So I rang him up and asked if we could meet because I had this sculpture of his and perhaps he wouldn't mind mending the tail because I didn't think I should tackle it. And that's how I met Eduardo. He wasn't nearly as frightening as I expected – it's just that he has this extraordinarily strong exterior. Rather alarming. I went there and looked at his work and we talked about the French sculptor César, who'd also done some birds. I found Paolozzi's early things very strong. In those days, funnily enough, he and Anthony Caro had something in common. That was before Caro changed, after going to America.

Frink's reservations, not fully stated but evident here, about the leading painter/

99

Horse and Rider, drawing (1977). This is unusual in giving so much landscape detail. Frink claimed she was unable to draw landscape, particularly trees.

sculptors of the twentieth century offer interesting clues about her own attitudes towards the business of making sculpture. It is possible to deduce that she thought their work was often interesting and attractive, but marginal because insufficiently plastic. If she makes an exception for Picasso's Shepherd *at Vallauris, this is clearly because she saw it as a direct, committed attempt to create a fully realised three-dimensional piece. The* Shepherd *does in fact bear a striking resemblance to some of her own standing male figures.*

I like some of Picasso's sculpture very much. When I was asked the other day to choose my favourite piece of sculpture, standing outside, somewhere in Europe, I chose Picasso's *Shepherd* in Vallauris. I think it's stunning. Some of his assemblages are brilliant, but there's something more serious about the *Shepherd*.

No one has ever done assemblages as cleverly as Picasso, but I think much of that stuff which is done now is very dreary. It has no wit at all; it's just broken-up stuff. Junk sculpture is really not very alluring because we're surrounded by junk anyway. I think it takes a very special talent to put it all together and create something of interest.

I'm not mad about Matisse's sculpture. I do find some of Miró's wild and

100

wonderful, but I didn't discover it till quite late. Max Ernst is a clever artist of his type: he's quite good as stringing things together, but his work isn't something that really appeals to me.

The fact that she did not want to work as they did in no way prevented Frink from taking an interest, often surprisingly sympathetic, in the work of avant-garde contemporaries. She was, however, quite certain that nearly all their activity was of a very different sort from her own. Essentially, I think, she would have liked to see it described by a different word: the fact that it was called 'sculpture' was, for her, an unfortunate historical accident.

I find some of Anish Kapoor's work seriously different. I don't like everything he does, but I can more or less see what he's up to. What I like, I like a lot. I was very glad when he got the Turner Prize. And I'm fascinated by Richard Long and Andy Goldsworthy, though I'm still not sure if their work is sculpture in the true sense of the word. In a sense, it's very ephemeral stuff. It disappears; it's not meant to last. Very different from what I do, because my work is made of bronze, and is therefore likely to be around for a very long time. Yet I have to say that I'm not really bothered if it is or isn't. I'm not consciously working for posterity – I never have done. You don't know what people in the future might think. They might consign all one's bronzes to a dump, or melt them down.

My own interest in what Richard Long and Andy Goldsworthy do is linked to my fascination with things like standing stones and ley lines. It's not sculpture as such; it's reshaping the landscape. And I appreciate it in those terms.

For me, the work of Damien Hirst and some of his contemporaries doesn't arouse interest in quite the same way. I feel it's all been done before. Perhaps I'd be more fascinated if it wasn't described as sculpture, but labelled as something quite different. Nor am I really interested in performance art, or very much in conceptual art. I can see that it does have a certain intellectual interest, but I don't call it sculpture.

Though Frink had many friends among painters, it is clear that, until quite a late stage in her career, she felt a certain detachment from the art of painting itself. She had tried it when she first went to art school at Guildford, and had decided it was not her vocation. It was only during the very last years of her career that she began

With one of the Hungarian vizslas, Woolland, 1980s.

101

making large-scale coloured drawings, and then, for a brief period, cut-out coloured figures in hardboard, on the scale of life or larger. Even though the latter were obviously 'painted surfaces', she remained uncertain in her own mind what their relationship to painting as an art form really was.

Painters, therefore, were people she valued as part of a social context, not individuals with whom she could exchange ideas or information.

One painter I loved was William Scott – I found him very good company and very amusing. Like the sculptor F. E. McWilliam, he was a Northern Irishman. I felt very sad for William when he was left out of the big British Painting show at the Royal Academy, which was held just before he died. Why not put him in, when so many lesser artists were included? Being omitted really knocked him. He wasn't well at the time – he had bad ulcers – and it really knocked him for six. Often that kind of thing is just a question of two people's opinion, and it can have terrible effects.

I probably knew more painters than sculptors in my early art-school days. Ceri Richards was a great friend. I liked his work and I liked him. He was large – a wonderful-looking, square Welshman, rather gentle. He was on the staff at Chelsea, as were Julian Trevelyan, Mary Fedden, all those people.

At about the same time, though they weren't teachers, I got to know Lucian Freud and Francis Bacon. Everyone was mad about Lucian, but I found him quite terrifying, I don't know why. He was nervous-making. Perhaps it was his eyes – they used to dart about. Francis I found absolutely marvellous, with a terrific sense of humour. I used to go to the Colony Room with him, and the French Pub, in Soho. In addition, I admired Francis's work; I found it probably the most powerful being done by any contemporary painter. I also saw John Minton, and Colquhoun and MacBride – the two Roberts. And Michael Andrews. I think I liked Michael Andrews's early work better than what he's doing now. I find the new stuff very photographic, almost Super Realist.

The painters divided into the Soho lot and the Fulham Road lot. The central figures in the Fulham Road group were the Moynihans, Rodrigo and Eleanor, who lived in Old Church Street, and were extremely nice to young artists. We all used to go back there after an evening at the public. Eleanor was marvellous: she was always cooking up sausages and mash.

Seated Baboon, bronze (1989). Frink was fascinated by the social hierarchies established amongst groups of baboons.

VI

In this final section I have brought together most of Elisabeth Frink's comments about her own work. There were a number of ideas she constantly reverted to — her preference for the male rather than the female image, for example, and her tendency to work in series. This tendency, in turn, she linked to a constant search for archetypal images — in fact, the whole instinctive thrust which made her a kind of belated Symbolist.

I don't find the female form the slightest bit interesting to sculpt. I can appreciate its beauty, but it hasn't got the structure. It doesn't supply the formula I need as a vehicle for my ideas. I enjoy looking at a male figure much more than at a female. It's not that I don't admire women, but their bodies are not suitable for what I have to say. And I don't do clothed figures. Cloth is very difficult to organise, and what kind of clothing are you going to use? Are you going to do today, or yesterday?

It has been said that Frink's early birds and birdmen are very much creatures of their time. She herself would have accepted this as being broadly true, though she would at the same time have rejected any pejorative implication. She understood that their aptness to the historical moment had undoubtedly played a role in winning her early recognition. She tended to stress purely personal influences — childhood and adolescence in Suffolk, and the impact made by contemporary events, as opposed to literary or mythological source material.

I suppose most of my early pieces — bird forms and birdmen — started with being brought up in the country, where I was surrounded with birds. I got very

Riace Bronzes I–IV (1986–9). These were inspired by two fifth-century Greek statues of warriors found in the sea off southern Italy.

105

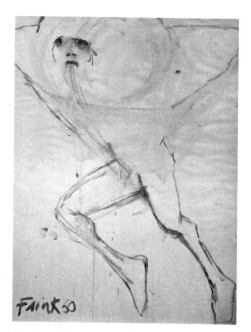

Birdman, drawing (1950) – the beginning of a long preoccupation with this theme. Frink *c.* 1964–5, photographed by Edward Pool.

Blind Beggar and His Dog, plaster for bronze (1957) – commissioned by Bethnal Green Borough Council.

106

interested in ravens and crows as a shape – sharp-beaked, splintery-type birds – and I think all my imagery was already there when I went to art school.

Even before that, however, I had been making strange, rather Germanic drawings, which went back to my efforts with Roddy, when I first started to take art seriously. I did a whole series of the Apocalypse, with strange, skeletal men on horseback, and the horses were skeletal as well. These were very tied up with the war – with Belsen. One was very conscious of the horrors of the war, chiefly through what was shown in the cinema. Not that I had been through horrors myself, but in 1945 they became known to people generally.

I had a little show of these early drawings at Heffer's bookshop in Cambridge, with a whole lot of other contemporary people. It was arranged by Bryan Robertson, who was later to be the director of the Whitechapel Art Gallery: he was then up at the university, and just a few years older than me. He was in his early twenties, and I was eighteen. There was a nice man in Suffolk, a banker called Brandt – the brother of the photographer Bill Brandt – who thought some of these early drawings were interesting and bought a few.

Nevertheless, though I started off doing images like that, when I got to Chelsea I chose to sculpt rather than to draw or to paint because I found it more sympathetic. The forms I sculpted were the ones which were most natural to me – animal and bird forms from Suffolk. However, I changed them enormously because they became much more like something else. They turned, almost, into a sort of bird-madness: quite fearsome, I think. Probably they were influenced by the aeroplanes I saw in the war – the equation was aeroplanes, flying machines, flying men, birdmen. I'm sure that was it. But the element of war angst was something that was over very quickly, both for me and for the other sculptors of the period. It's rather boring to hear so much about it now, when people talk about the sculpture of the 1950s. We were all on to something else by then.

People find it tempting to say that my birdmen stemmed from the Icarus legend, but that's not really true either. They came much more from reading about an extraordinary Frenchman called Valentin, who used to jump out of aeroplanes wearing his own pair of wings. There was another sculptor at the same time as me, César, working not in London but in Paris, who was doing sculptures based on Valentin. They were totally different from mine, because he worked in wax, not in plaster.

107

I've always worked in plaster, rather than in wax or clay – from the time I first went to Chelsea. It was Bernard Meadows, who was teaching there, who really got me into plaster. And by that time I already knew something about Giacometti, who used plaster, although of course he got a very different result from me. My birds and birdmen were built up on an armature, and then carved back, using chisels and choppers and all sorts of implements. In those days I also used to pick up bits of discarded plaster, and reuse them welded together with new material. That's why the effect is so splintery. The early imagery was a combination of the country, animals and the war.

But if, as people have said, and as I've just said, there was an echo of the war in my work, I very quickly forgot it. I was totally apolitical in that period. I never thought about politics in relation to humanity, to human beings, until the 1960s. While I knew about Fascism, obviously, I was totally unaware of Communism.

When I left art school, what I hoped for was quite simple: I wanted to be able to do my work, earn some money and have exhibitions. In that sense I was quite ambitious. I wanted to improve, to get better at what I did. I never thought particularly about marriage, though in fact I got married quite soon: it rather took me by surprise. When I left, I got a studio in Park Walk, between the King's Road and the Fulham Road, which was a little bigger than my kitchen here at Woolland. It was tall – very high – and about twelve foot by ten foot, and the rent was two pounds ten shillings a week. I did a lot of work there, and though I was quite normal and had various boyfriends, I lived the most essential part of my life in my mind. I just ignored what was happening in the world – world affairs after the war – because I was so determined to make art. I was already working life size. At the end of my time at Chelsea I'd already been working quite big, using the model. In 1954, soon after I left Chelsea, I showed in the open-air sculpture exhibition in Holland Park.

Frink's attitudes towards the public were perhaps more élitist than her reputation – that of successful communicator, almost a populist – suggests. For her, I think, there was a key difference between sculpture and other manifestations of visual art, which was that the audience did not always choose to look at sculpture. When it was outdoors, in some public place, they encountered it as part of the everyday

Horse and Rider, bronze (1974). This piece in Dover Street, commissioned by Trafalgar House, is now one of London's most familiar Public sculptures. Because the neighbouring building is occupied by Aeroflot, the sculpture became – to Frink's amusement – a focal point for political demonstrations.

109

environment. For the modern artist, working in a divided and fragmented culture, this situation raised special problems – questions of integrity, but also questions of tact.

I do what I do because I want to do it. I don't think I make any allowances for the fact that the public perhaps might not like it. Because obviously, if I've got an idea, I want to do it. I'm not sure if an artist should be absolutely accessible to everyone. If it so happens that my work is in fact accessible, and a lot of other people's isn't, I don't want to be arrogant about that.

The truth is, of course, that you envisage an audience, if you're a sculptor, the moment you put your work outside, the moment you have a work outside. And as soon as you become publicly known, you begin to think about the people who are going to respond to your work. But you don't change direction just to get a particular sort of response. You have to be very careful. In one sense, you can go too far to meet the expectations of the audience. On the other, you can cut them out altogether, saying, 'They can take what I've done, or leave it.' It's a very difficult path to tread.

I'm still not sure how far the artist owes the public some sort of communication. I know that members of the public complain bitterly and often that they don't understand some of the art that's going on in public places. I don't know if that's because they're not trying. In England there's never been a real tradition of sculpture in public. People don't know how to approach it really. I think that's got a lot to do with it. I'm pleased if my work is accessible, but I don't think it has to be.

Though Frink undertook numerous public commissions in the course of her career, she was always very firm about the need to retain complete creative independence. She avoided anything which strayed from what she saw as her own range of imagery – hence her determination to avoid doing full-length portrait statues. It is, however, a great pity that she did not live to complete the projected sculpture of Shakespeare she mentions here. The idea of an English equivalent of Rodin's Balzac *is a tantalising one.*

Mostly I've managed to do commissions choosing my own subject. My feeling now, after having done a number of public commissions, is that I'd much rather somebody came to see me and said, 'I like this set of heads or that set of figures;

and they'd suit the site I have in mind.' I think it's very difficult doing something specifically. I don't mind doing it, however, as long as I have a totally free hand.

I've only done one commission that was totally unsatisfactory — that was for the Carlton Tower Hotel, and the reason it doesn't work is that what I did was more or less dictated to me by the building. I know many architects — Denys Lasdun is one of them — are totally against having sculpture on their buildings. They don't want stuff clashing with their own forms. In a way I agree with them. I think it's very difficult to put a piece of sculpture actually on a building. The best relationship is when they're nearby, complementary to the architecture, but not part of the building as such.

My first public commission was when the architects Yorke, Rosenberg and Mardell commissioned me to do a *Blind Beggar and His Dog* for Bethnal Green. The moving spirit was Eugene Rosenberg, who was a terrific collector and patron of the arts. It's now not in its original place because it was vandalised. It spent some time in the local public library, and then was pushed out again somewhere. But it's still in Bethnal Green.

Then I did a small *Wild Boar* for Harlow New Town, and I've done other things for London sites. I suppose the best known is the *Horse* outside the Aeroflot building in Piccadilly. That was commissioned by Nigel Broakes of Trafalgar House. My idea was that there hadn't been a public sculpture of a horse in London for a long time. The funny thing is that people now associate it with the Russians. It's often chosen as a starting point for demonstrations, instead of the Russian Embassy in Kensington.

In addition, there is the *Shepherd and His Flock* in Paternoster Square, surrounded by very ugly buildings, and the *Eagle Squadrons Monument* near the American Embassy, which commemorates the American airmen who came over here to fight because of the war. I suppose, because of its subject, it's a slight throwback to my early sculptures of birds.

One thing I've always avoided is portrait statues: I don't do that sort of sculpture. Yet, having said this, I have taken on the idea of doing a large Shakespeare for Sam Wanamaker's rebuilt Globe Theatre. In my mind's eye I see something slightly Balzacian about it — I mean, I'm thinking of doing a piece a bit like Rodin's sculpture of Balzac in Paris.

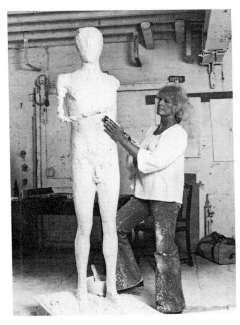

With the figure of the shepherd for the *Paternoster* group, Paternoster Square, London, 1973. The complete group shows a shepherd and his flock.

111

112

Religious commissions did, however, enjoy a special place in Frink's œuvre. Despite the fact that she had severed her connection with organised religion, she was still essentially a believer, and the iconography of the Christian faith remained meaningful for her. In particular, she was able to assimilate her own feeling for heroic male figures with the image of the crucified or risen Christ. Her last major commission, the Risen Christ *for Liverpool, certainly had deep personal significance.*

Church commissions are different from other public commissions. During my career I've done a lot of work for churches, and I'm working on a big *Risen Christ* for Liverpool just at the moment. One of my earliest church pieces is the *Eagle Lectern* for Coventry, but that wasn't specifically religious. I did other bits and pieces for Coventry as well – for instance the *Flame of the Holy Spirit* in copper, very high up, and a copper bishop's mitre. It was the only time I've worked in copper – I've never done it again.

After that I did a very big *Crucifixion* for a Catholic church in Belfast, a standing figure. It's very simple, almost two-dimensional, because it has to be carried in procession. The idea of Christ as a cross, with nothing attached: I love that idea. At about the same time – 1964 – I did another big Christ for a Catholic church in Solihull, a *Risen Christ*, the predecessor of the one I'm doing now. I also did a head of Christ I rather like for a church in Basingstoke, a very contemplative piece.

The *Madonna* for Salisbury Cathedral Close was a one-off – because it's a female figure and because it's draped. Doing the drapery was very difficult. But it was a fascinating job because of where it is.

What I really enjoy, however, is doing Crucifixions and figures of Christ. It's an enormous challenge, doing something which has already been done so often in the last two thousand years. There are already so many different interpretations, yet one goes into it thinking that one might possibly find another aspect.

The big figure I'm working on now started with the Liverpool Cathedral committee wanting to have a Christ on the façade of the building, above the west door. Apparently before they asked me they'd had a competition from which they made a short list of about six sculptors, but they weren't happy with any of the designs. So they explained the situation to me and asked if I would

Working on the shepherd for the *Paternoster* group, 1973.

113

114

be interested, which of course I was, because here was this really fantastic opportunity to do something large for an important building. So that's how it started.

I have to admit that I'd always assumed that the Anglican cathedral in Liverpool was rather boring. All I knew was that it was a large sandstone building by Giles Gilbert Scott, built during the last hundred years. I'd never even seen photographs of it. I changed my mind immediately I went there because it really is very beautiful, with enormous spaces inside.

The site was already chosen, which in a way made life very difficult for me, as the figure starts with its feet already twenty feet above the ground, so that you have to allow for all sorts of optical distortions when you're immediately underneath it. On the other hand, people also approach it from afar. I've never had to deal with problems of this type before, and I find them fascinating. Sometimes I'll lie down on the floor of the studio and look up at the figure to get the right perspective. That sort of thing is fun.

I wanted it to be a very simple, primitive figure. The one thing I didn't want was the usual limp Christ figure, and I didn't want drapes or any clothing at all. I immediately made this quite clear to the Dean, and of course he was thrilled because what he'd had in mind all along was a very big, simple Christ. I did some drawings to show him and he was thrilled. They were very like the big figure you see in the studio – almost Greek *kouros* figures. 'Here I am, back from the dead!' That's what he's saying, really.

I suppose it's taken me three months to get it nearly finished. I had the armature made back in the summer and I started again in September [1992]. I think I can say it's been done since September. It's been slightly more rapid than my usual rate of work because for the first time I took on an assistant because of the size and the carrying of buckets of plaster. He's not a trained sculptor but a young architect. Sometimes when I've put on too much plaster he helps me to hack it off, but I always do the finishing, because after all the last word on every surface of the figure has to be mine.

The fact that my assistant isn't a sculptor was pretty much a matter of chance, but I think it's worked out very well because, being a trained architect, he has a sense of scale. I find it's a very good arrangement.

For me this resurrected Christ definitely has a personal meaning, similar to

Walking Madonna, bronze (1981). The photograph shows the sculpture being lowered into place in Salisbury Cathedral Close.

115

that of the *Green Man* heads. They all symbolise a rebirth, a renewal of spirit and mind. I think at the moment it's still probably a little bit too stern. I think it will possibly have a small beard on the chin. My son has a very sculptural face, and he has a little beard. I shall probably use his head as a model.

I imagine a lot of people will say that the Christ is a bit too stern, and not compassionate enough. But then I think you also have to be very careful. When Christ came back from the dead, it says in the creed, 'He was crucified and buried, and on the third day he rose again [from the dead], and ascended into Heaven and sat on the right hand of God the Father. From thence he shall come to judge the quick and the dead.' In fact, he may be a redeemer, the risen Christ, but he has also come to judge us. So I think a stern quality is not out of the way. He is also in judgement even though his hands are out, which people will tend to interpret as a welcoming gesture. I didn't want his hands loose and hanging.

I've decided against having his eyes looking down, because if you do that from such a height they look almost closed. They're going to be wide open and looking straight ahead. I think there's a faint pre-Columbian echo in the figure as well as something early Greek. I was very keen to get that very big, simple quality. I think I'm working much more now towards a very big simplicity. Much greater simplicity in the planes of the sculpture, but the surfaces will all be slightly textured, because I love working them afterwards with the chisel. I think when the bronze is up, whatever the colour (which I haven't quite decided yet), these marks will reflect the light.

Granted Frink's involvement with church commissions, it is doubly fascinating that she cites the Judas *of 1963 as a key work in her early development. Her account of this figure, and of the* Dying King, *demonstrates the characteristically 'mixed' nature of her creative process. Internal necessity – the desire to create a sculpture of a particular sort – was often reinforced by purely external circumstances: President Kennedy's assassination, or the fact that she had recently seen Olivier's film of Shakespeare's* Richard III.

The early *Judas* is one of my most interesting pieces – or that's how I always think of it. Getting to a piece like that is a gradual process, an idea starts way back. You see something, you like a face or a figure, and you really want to nail

In the studio with the almost completed plaster of the *Risen Christ* for Sir Giles Gilbert Scott's Anglican cathedral in Liverpool, 1992.

116

117

118

it, you want to give it some source in your own mind. For example, with *Judas* I wanted to do this massive figure, and I wanted a figure which was fending off some kind of attack. And the more the idea developed, the more it became for me a figure of betrayal — it was very strange. Ideas often come in a very cock-eyed fashion. Judas is quite a strong figure, but he also has a weakness about him. With his arm out, he's making a gesture of invitation, yet fending you off at the same time. Also, he's blinded. It's the first piece of sculpture I made with shades over the eyes, and in that sense it leads on to the *Goggle Heads*. It's a figure I'm deeply attached to because it marked a major change in my work. I did it at the same time as I made a couple of smaller groups of assassins. Those were associated in my mind with the Kennedy assassination.

The *Dying King*, with the *Judas*, is one of the two key pieces in my 1960s work. He's dying on a battlefield. The idea came from seeing a film which showed Richard III being killed in battle, stabbed to death as he puts his arm up to fend his attackers off. And I'd been going round churches two or three days earlier, looking at the figures on medieval tombs, which I found quite wonderful. So it's also a crusader figure on a tomb. But while the idea I had for *Judas* went on and developed into the *Goggle Heads*, I didn't develop a line from the *Dying King*. The idea sort of stopped.

The fact that Frink so often reverted to the Goggle Heads *in conversation indicates clearly that they had a strongly personal meaning for her. Yet they are among the most ambiguous and controversial of her works. Hostile critics often read them as being political statements of a rather naïve sort — 'against' tyranny, 'for' liberty and democracy — things very much in line with Frink's support for organisations such as Amnesty International. Matters are not that simple — they were inspired, as she says, by photographs of some of the Algerian leaders who took over power after the Algerian War of Independence, and thus cannot in fact be read as emblems of opposition to colonialism. Rather, they offer a comment on what the Third World has tended to make of itself after the colonial powers have withdrawn.*

I think my first fully conscious comments on the world's inhumanity were the *Goggle Heads*. When I moved to France I got interested in the Algerian War, which was then only just over. It still rumbled away, the horror of it. You met Pieds Noirs down there in the Cevennes — French settlers who had had to leave

Green Man, drawing (1991). Frink's late drawings are always extremely bold in style.

119

Algeria. Very nice people they were, and wonderful farmers. What really triggered the series were some rather extraordinary photographs of people like General Oufkir. They all hid behind dark glasses, and these became a symbol of evil for me. The title *Goggle Heads* was rather facetious, a way of dealing with the horror of the imagery. At that time photographs played an important part in suggesting my images. It was a great era for photo-journalism, and I used to make collections of photographs taken from magazines. All the action photographers they used had originally been war photographers.

Like many successful artists — and indeed like many successful creative writers — Frink felt that her work was often misread, even by those who appeared to be most enthusiastic about it. In her case, it was the representations of animals (her most popular works) that were especially apt to be misconstrued.

I always try to explain that I haven't done a great many animals — that I'm not in fact an animal sculptor. If you love animals you have to have some sort of sympathy with the way they are or exist, and how we treat them. If I'm sculpturing animals I don't want to oversentimentalise them because one can be very sentimental about that part of our life. I'd find it a very sad life without animals: we need them, that's the awful thing. I think man is dependent on animals and this dependency puts an awful responsibility on the animal: they have to lump it. Your dog is entirely dependent on you — your needs, your whims, how you are feeling. For this he gives you undying devotion. It's an extraordinary relationship. I find it so strange that in a sense I want to distance myself a tiny bit from it when I'm doing sculpture.

Once I've seen an animal I have a vision of it in my mind, because I do have a very photographic memory. When I saw the water-buffalo, which I afterwards did for the Hong Kong and Shanghai Bank, I looked at them for a very long time — enough to get them into my retina, recorded. I can remember faces in the same way, minutely. I can see someone very briefly — not even meet them — and I'll still remember that face. I think I look at things very specifically. And I look at animals in very much that way and record them for myself.

This is another reason why I'm not a true animal sculptor. The animals I make are far more what I feel about them than what they are in real life. I'm

Eagle Squadrons Monument, Grosvenor Square. This commemorates the American airmen who came over to fight in the RAF during the Second World War.

121

imprecise about the muscles and the blood vessels, which is what a lot of academic sculptors care about. I'm much more interested in the spirit of the animal. I get into the inside of the animal, and the outside takes care of itself.

Frink's description of the evolution of her sculptures of wild boars gives an especially clear picture of her creative process.

One of the reasons I started sculpting boars* was that when I lived in France, in the Cevennes, we were surrounded by woods and we could actually see wild boars, especially at night. On moonlit nights they'd be making their passages down to the Camargue. They're very fascinating, shy creatures. I was attracted more by their emblematic than by their sculptural qualities. Much of my work is based on that — the combination of something past, the Celtic element, something now, and something which might possibly be in the future. My various sources have been quite precise, but they've turned into something else *en route*. There's an accumulation of ideas. If you think about something like a wild boar it brings together a whole lot of new ideas and feelings. An image of a boar becomes a place to put an idea or a feeling, and my work is mainly through feeling. Observation does come into it as well, naturally, but I use observation to create a shell for whatever feeling you're doing.

The strongly metaphorical element in much of Frink's work can be seen particularly clearly in her small series entitled The Mirages. *They are, as she says, extremely close to abstraction, in comparison with the rest of her work.*

The Mirages — that was a strange theme. It really came from going to visit the Camargue for quite long periods. In the very hot weather people on horseback, or birds — flamingos in the distance — used to assume these strange, stalking shapes, floating, broken up by the distance. I think at the time I was trying to do something which was part bird, part stalking beast, but not entirely either. I just did three or four big ones and a series of small ones. They're fairly abstract, compared with what I usually did.

Water-buffaloes, bronze (1987) — commissioned for Sir Norman Foster's Hongkong and Shanghai Bank.

---

*This is not quite accurate. Frink made one or two images of boars *before* she moved to France. ELS

Frink's heads, the Desert Heads *in particular, court abstraction in a different way, through their use of extremely simplified and generalised forms. For Frink, these heads were male, and closely connected to her full-length male figures. Outside observers sometimes perceived in them a resemblance to Frink herself.*

I called the *Desert Heads* that because I connected them with the feeling that I got in the desert in Tunisia. They portray individuals and also they go together collectively. The way I worked on them was in pairs, moving from one to the other. As I moved to the second pair they became a bit more precise, a bit punchier. For me, the image of the head is a good place to put ideas and sensations. After all, everything goes on in your head. If you think of past civilisations, there are marvellous head sculptures.

Heads have always been very important to me as vehicles for sculpture. A head is infinitely variable. It's complicated, and it's extremely emotional. Everyone's emotions are in their face. It's not surprising that there are sculptures of massive heads going way back, or that lots of other artists besides myself have found the subject fascinating. I'm already thinking about the next lot.

Frink's many representations of the male nude culminated in the four Riace Warriors, *which were inspired by two fifth-century* B.C. *Greek sculptures discovered in the 1970s in the sea off southern Italy. These Greek sculptures are notable for the absence of the classical calm so often attributed by scholars to the art of this period – they have a disconcerting air of savagery, combined with unease. For Frink, the discovery confirmed feelings she already had about the real nature of ancient sculpture. It was as if the Greeks had anticipated ideas that she had formulated independently.*

I remember reading about the Riace warriors – how they were found in the sea off Calabria and brought up to the surface. Then I remember them being on show in Florence. The original figures are very beautiful, but also very sinister, and that is what they are supposed to be.

When we were both doing a film together I talked to Peter Levi, who is a Greek scholar, and he explained their meaning: the fact that these were warriors who would go out and fight your battles for you, mercenaries, but in return they had to have certain sacrifices made to them. In other words, they

Desert Quartet, bronze patinated white (1989) – inspired by a visit to the Tunisian desert.

125

were thugs. Even though I don't particularly like sinister things, thuggishness is a bit of a preoccupation with me. It all hinges on my humanitarian sentiments. And it all fits in with the context: after all, you only have to read the Greek myths, or the plays of the great Greek dramatists, to understand that this was a society which led a fairly violent life.

I was fascinated by the fact that the figures had these two sides to them, and making new versions seemed like a marvellous idea, one I really wanted to tackle. I still don't think I've quite finished with it. In the set of *Riace Warriors* I've recently had cast I used different-coloured patinas to put masks on the figures. It's a way of showing that their beauty in a sense hides what they are up to.

What I've always said about my figures, and I think it's true, is that they're nothing to do with any known myth. For instance, they're not really to do with the Greek myths, although I've illustrated those, and they're not to do with any known myth that you've read about. Yet they are mythical – they're part of our past. They're nothing to do with what I'm seeing now or looking at. They're to do with our collective past, but they're also a part of today's world. The *Riace Warriors* could be translated into something else. It depends on the viewer. The idea is that something might be bursting out of these people. They're restraining or constraining vessels of skin and muscle and sinew which something else might possibly burst out of – that's the feeling I want to get. It's interesting how much you can put into a piece of sculpture, and how it changes as you build it up. Often they're accidental changes which may suggest something else, so that you start to push things in another direction. It's all very flexible.

The War Horse – *Frink's second-to-last major sculpture (much of the work on it was done after the onset of her illness) – was, as she implies, a reversion to her beginnings as an artist, since the horse of Verrocchio's* Colleoni Monument *was very visibly one of her chief sources of inspiration for the piece. She modernised Verrocchio's approach in a characteristic way, by changing the focus: this is no longer a beast mastered by a rider, but one which exists independently. At the same time, however, she wanted to introduce the idea that this horse had suffered in the service of man. There are a number of drawings, slightly earlier than the* War Horse *in date, which show*

The studio at Woolland, with the re-used carcass set up for work on the *War Horse* (1991).

126

wounded and bleeding horses. Generally only the head of the horse is shown, with blood running down its cheek or muzzle. These horses, too, wait passively, rather than reacting violently to suffering.

The idea for the *War Horse* started about the time of the Gulf War. I wanted to do a huge animal, and to say something more about the horse's relationship to man – the way the horse has carried men through countless battles. It's an aspect of the relationship I found upsetting, but I also found it inspiring. I remember someone saying to me, 'Are you going to do any more life-size horses?' and I remember replying, 'Yes, but not in any way like the previous ones.' The ones that everyone remembers are either the horse in Piccadilly, which was done quite a long time ago now, or the one in front of the racecourse at Goodwood, which is a sort of thoroughbred, though I suppose the race-going public wouldn't consider it much of a racehorse, but that's the way they are and that's the way I am.

I knew that I wanted to do a very different horse. So I said it would be a war horse, and large, and they said, 'Oh, you mean a shire horse?' Well, I didn't mean a shire horse either, because, though it is big like a shire horse, it's not like a working horse, it's something different. But there again it's the inside, the spirit of this horse that I was really interested in. I'd been just longing to do a really big chunky horse.

Things of that kind can be rooted very far back in your career. The first what I'd call really big monumental sculpture I ever saw was the *Colleoni Monument* in Venice, at the age of seventeen. I often get my ideas a long time beforehand, and stow them away. A moment comes when you think, 'Now there's an idea I want to do.'

For the *War Horse* I began by making two small models, which gave me an idea of the volume. One consideration was that I had an old plaster lying about outside, left over from one of my older horses – just the body. I got that remounted, because it saved me an awful lot of time. You have to think about things like that, if you don't have assistants. I recycle a lot of the old plasters I have lying around, left over from sculptures I've finished with. In this case I had this huge body of a horse, and I thought, 'Now's the time, before it disintegrates any further, to get that set up.' So inside the *War Horse* there's another, quite different horse. My idea was to do a strong chunky animal, just standing there, almost as if it was wounded, but not plunging round in a hysterical way. The idea carried me through my operation, and I worked on it again afterwards. It was wonderful to have it there to come back to.

The Duchess of Devonshire saw it, and decided it would be perfect for Chatsworth, up at the end of the long canal, so she persuaded the trustees to buy it. Her husband didn't see it until it was actually installed. He came back that very evening from London. Fortunately he thought it was just right for the spot.

To the end of her life, Frink's attention remained fixed on the future, rather than the past. In particular, she had many plans for new sculptures. More and more, as can be seen from her comments here, she thought of her work as a vehicle for social and ethical ideas. Nevertheless she was not content with the idea alone – she was always in search of a way of expressing it which would be formally complete. This is one of the main points of difference between her work and that of a younger generation of sculptors who had turned their backs on supposed formalism in order to try and express moral and political standpoints.

My next theme, which I'm really anxious to get into quite soon, is this composition I already did several paintings of for my last exhibition. I want to do a sculpture showing a seated man with a seated baboon, posed as though they were having a conversation. I haven't quite worked it out yet – how to get it all hanging together. Translating things into the round is going to be quite difficult. I'll need a space to put the two figures in, and maybe I'll need an additional object. I might have a bench, or something like that.

I want to do it because I think it's an interesting relationship. A baboon is an animal with a fascinating family life. Groups of baboons observe a very strict hierarchy – whereas man goes over the top and breaks the rules. It's almost a criticism of the man by the baboon that I want to imply. The animal kingdom has strict parameters; we human beings are supposed to have them, but of course we don't. Animals don't murder in the way that we do, wantonly. They kill to eat, or to defend themselves and their young. Man goes further than that, and the contrast is what I'd like to express.

129

Portrait of Sir John Pope-Hennessy (1975) —
commissioned by the British Museum, of
which Frink was for a long time a trustee.

*Frink was a slightly reluctant but excellent portraitist — she gives the reasons for her
reluctance here. It is the one department of her work where it is possible to detect a
faint kinship to Epstein, though there is perhaps an even closer resemblance to the
portraits done by the Italian sculptors Marini and Manzù, which, in turn, are based
on Etruscan terracotta heads of the fourth century B.C. and later. It is not surprising
that all her sitters were men, given her established preference for the male image. The
sole exception is her remarkable self-portrait. I believe this was inspired by a request
from myself, as co-curator (with Sean Kelly) of an exhibition of contemporary self-
portraits first shown at the Art-Site Gallery in Bath, and later circulated to a number
of other museums and galleries. There are two striking things about this portrait: first,
its completely objective assessment of her own appearance — it is very 'like' without
being at all romanticised — and secondly, the slightly hesitant sensitivity which it
seems to reveal. Some people describe Elisabeth Frink as being slightly formidable.
That quality is not apparent here.*

Portraits are extremely exacting to do. If I have to do one I'm apt to think I
really don't in fact want to do it. Mainly, I suppose, because you have to please
so many people. Or perhaps you don't actually have to, but you do try. It's got to
be an individual, but it's also my idea of what they look like. You want to make
something of your own out of it, something in its own right. So you want to
turn it into something a bit more than a straightforward likeness. One thing
that always happens is that you get people far too late, when they're too mature.
Sometimes you feel it's a shame that you haven't got them ten years earlier.
And the sitters, however modest they are, or lacking in vanity, always worry. I
find they worry terribly: I suppose that's natural, really. And people close to
them worry. I remember Helen Hamlyn, Paul Hamlyn's wife, getting quite
anxious. She used to bring me little snapshots, her favourite photos of Paul, and
that wasn't at all how I saw him.

One terrible disadvantage for a portrait sculptor is the fact that the sitter can
see everything you do — you're turning the head round all the time. A painter
can put the canvas up and hide behind it. The sitter need never see the canvas if
the artist doesn't want to show it to him. Whereas when you're doing a
sculpture the sitter sees it all the time, and I suppose it's quite alarming for
him.

130

I do like the sitters to talk. I don't like them to be absolutely rigid because they get very unrelaxed. I've been very lucky in that sense. I've sculpted some very interesting people and they've all chattered away. And I've learned a lot.

I first did portraits when I was still at Chelsea – Breon O'Casey, the painter and jeweller, son of Sean O'Casey. My dentist. An American painter called Roger Garth. Then I stopped, and when I came back from France I started again. I did John Pope-Hennessy, and the composer William Walton, and a whole lot more.

John Pope-Hennessy's head fascinated me because it had this extraordinary quality – this taut skin. He was really charming because he always assumed that I knew nearly as much history of art as he did. He once said to me, 'Oh, I was in the Uffizi the other day, and you know there's that painting as you come down the stairs, well now of course they've moved it and put it somewhere else.' And I had to pretend I knew what he was talking about. He always used to talk about a place called 'Millan'. 'Where's Millan?' I'd think to myself. It took a long time to dawn that what he meant was Milan.

William Walton was equally fascinating to do. I got on very well with him and he was extremely witty about other people – very witty, sharp. He talked about the Sitwells. About other composers – things in the past. His brain was extremely sharp.

I've made some very good friends through doing portraits. One was Alec Guinness, though he didn't like sitting at all. Perhaps he's so enigmatic that he doesn't, himself, really know who he is at any given moment. The best times were when we'd finished a sitting. We used to have lunch together, and then he was marvellous.

Georg Solti was a difficult experience. It was like trying to do a head in a desert storm, because he never had enough time to sit. He came down here twice, and that was fine. Then I made a terrible mistake, and said I'd bring the head up to London – portraits are the one thing I do in clay, not in plaster. I ended up in a basement, and he was surrounded by men all bowing and scraping, and rushing around and screaming 'Maestro!' here and 'Maestro!' there. Finally he sat down and pulled out a score and said, 'You don't mind if I go through this, do you? It's *The Messiah*, and I'm off to Chicago tomorrow, and I've never conducted it before.' I said, 'It isn't very easy because what I've got is

Portrait of Sir William Walton (1976) – commissioned by the Royal Festival Hall.

131

a face turned downward, looking at a score.' And he said, 'I can hold my head up!' But of course the result was that he was tense inside, rather than relaxed. I had to take the head home and finish it off without him.

One thing I regret now is that I didn't get into doing portraits of my family. I don't know what the reason for that was. I wish I'd done a head of my son when he was a child. I only did a portrait when he was older. If you look, for instance, at Epstein's heads of babies, they're absolutely remarkable. I love those sculptures.

Frink's drawings were, as she notes, popular and widely circulated. These sheets have a striking boldness, which comes partly from the fluidity of her whole process of draughtsmanship, but also from the way in which she tended to fill the entire sheet of paper. As she matured as an artist, her drawings grew steadily bolder – the search for the essential tended to rule out fine nuances. Very late drawings, in which brilliant colour is often paramount, seem to have gone most of the way towards becoming paintings. They demonstrate, more clearly and obviously than her sculptures, a hidden connection with German Expressionism.

Drawing for me is a way of sorting out my ideas. I like to draw on large sheets. That's why I could never cope with sketchbooks at art school. I go straight on to big paper. Nowadays I mostly draw in charcoal. Before that it was in ink and wash. I'm searching my mind for ideas I might use, but the drawings are also things in their own right. Thrusting out – going over the edge of the paper – parallels what I'm doing when I'm sculpting, creating the volume of say a male figure. What I want then is a dynamic from inside, pressing against the inside of the skin.

In drawing I don't think I ever want anything to be totally complete, and that applies to sculpture as well. I don't want the viewer to feel that that is everything there is to see. I always want to suggest a further state – a further state of mind or a further state of physicality. So the image is on the move, not completely static. I find this quite difficult to do, but it's my main aim, the one thing I desperately want. That's how one thing grows from another.

About two or three years ago I really began to feel the need to use colour. It coincided with my trip to Australia – the colour there just blows your mind, the

Working on her bust of Alec Guinness, 1983.

132

colour of the earth. I wanted very bright red earth colours, and blues – indigos. I'm still quite keen to use colour, but I'm not sure that I'd now go on in the same way. My move into colour in drawing was linked to my decision to use much more brilliant patination. The desire to do colour on paper is all tied up with the desire to do coloured patinas.

I think that when I was a very young artist I lived very much in my mind, and that is why I stopped drawing from life. I did a lot once, when I was starting out, but I stopped doing it because I found I wanted to look intensely, very intensely, at everything, without being distracted. I trained my eye to look, and retain images. I stored these images in my mind and then I'd go back to the studio and make the drawing. Whatever I draw, I don't deliberate. If the drawing doesn't work, I just tear it up. But now I wonder if I shouldn't go back to life drawing, do what they call a refresher course, because my figures have got so removed from real anatomy. In a sense I now remake anatomy to suit myself.

All my drawings are ideas which might lead up to sculpture, but they don't necessarily do so. The process is very important because it's a way of getting my ideas out on paper. But I've always liked drawing on a big scale. Therefore the notebook, sketchbook-type drawing was always absolutely out. I never kept a sketchbook even when I was a student, because I was completely incapable of doing so, and I remember that this used to be frowned on sometimes, because everybody else did it.

I have periods of drawing, when I draw things I think I might sculpt, then I have periods of actually doing sculpture. I don't generally do drawings and sculpture together, because the drawings, in that case, tend to get messed up. Up until now I've done everything in the same studio. What I do is to make a group of drawings, working up to the very edge of the paper, then I put them aside for a while in order to think about them.

My drawings have always sold well, and originally they were very cheap. They aren't expensive even now, really. I think the nice thing about drawings is that they're available to people who can't necessarily afford sculpture, and of course they're a very personal comment from the artist. Sculptors' drawings are more interesting than painters' drawings, usually because there's a bigger gap between them and the finished three-dimensional object. Yet they also tell you important things about the sculpture itself. One of the things I find fascinating about Giacometti's drawings, and also his paintings, is that they're so tremendously spacious.

Your way of drawing doesn't remain static. It changes as you develop. I find my own drawings are now much more direct. I block them out, and use lots of lines to suggest changes in texture.

Frink's prints are best thought of as an extension of her drawing process. Basically, though the techniques of print-making interested her, she was not fully engaged with them — they were very much a means to an end, and the resultant images are very close indeed to her drawings, differing only in being a little less spontaneous, a little more considered.

I did some lithographs at art school, but none of them survived. I think they were on very thin paper. I didn't tackle lithography again until I joined Curwen in the 1960s. I did my first lot of lithographs on stone with Stanley James around 1964. I love doing prints and every time I do some I think, 'This is exciting — why don't I do more?' At the same time I'm a bit reserved about it. I think it's a marvellous thing to have prints available, because it enables a lot of young people to build up a collection. And I also think that, just as long as the artist works on the plate himself or herself, it's an authentic medium.

However, I now find I prefer etching to lithography, because with etching you're actually dealing directly with the plate, working on it. I think it's a bit like sculpture, because it's quite direct. With lithography, things are actually quite complicated. I liked it when they told me all the things I could do, like floating ink on water and wax — I liked that better than straightforward lithography. But the problem with lithographs is that they have to keep going back into the press. You wipe the stone off, and then you pull something, and so on. That's something I find very teasing.

Book illustration was an occasional activity, only intermittently pursued. Frink brought to it her love of literature, but regarded commissions of this kind (which she never actively sought) as a minor diversion from her main business, producing sculpture on bronze.

The first illustrated book I did was *Aesop's Fables*. I really enjoyed that — it was a lovely thing to do, and it's still one of my favourite books. The commission came through Alistair McAlpine. I first met him when he was very young, shortly after he left school. Someone brought him round to my studio to look at my drawings, and he bought a few. Later he bought a great deal of my work, though he's just recently sold it when he left England and went to live abroad. Alistair was running a small venture with Waddington, producing books by artists. So we did *Aesop's Fables* and then Chaucer's *Canterbury Tales.* Then much later I did the *Greek Myths* for Longman – not a lot of books. I quite enjoy doing that sort of thing for a change, though it's easier to do the figures than their settings. I can't draw things like trees; I have to find my own convention for them.

Like all artists Frink was keenly interested in how her work was shown. The way her sculptures were displayed at Woolland was a demonstration of this interest, as was the fact that the arrangement was frequently changed, especially where the newer sculptures were concerned. One of her unfulfilled ambitions was to see her sculptures exhibited in an urban but still outdoor setting – that is, in the kind of spaces provided by a historic Italian town.

There are two ways of showing sculpture – or my sculpture. One is outside in a nice landscape, preferably not a formal garden, with trees and sky. Or else in a gallery situation. I like this for totally different reasons. Sculptures take on more concentrated energy in a gallery, when they're confined by big white walls. I rather like that. It puts my work in a new aspect.

The point about an exhibition is that it removes the surrounding clutter. I like to have very few pieces in a show. And I like to have key drawings in certain areas, where they don't interfere with the sculpture itself – I think that's important. Really what I need is space, uncluttered space.

I'm less and less into bases. They're a necessity for small pieces, because you've got to sit them on something – they can't just sit on the floor. Though, funnily enough, even that is not completely true. Some small sculptures *can* go on the floor. And I'm against bases for my big standing figures now.

In an exhibition, the lighting is very important. I had a brilliant man who lit my sculptures for my show in the Women's Museum at Washington. Another important things is that people must be able to go round the sculptures. They've got to be away from the walls.

I remember my early exhibitions as being messy, somehow, bitty. But from 1957 onwards I never had a bad space because I was showing with Waddington. I think museum display has had a big influence on the way private galleries show work, and that's not a bad thing.

One thing I'd like would be to have a large retrospective one day, somewhere outside. What I see in my mind's eye is somewhere where there's a lot of stone – ancient buildings. I'd like to see my work in an architectural setting, because I'm already used to seeing it in a green landscape. I really hanker for something much more architectural than the space we have here in Dorset – a place where people walk, and go about their daily business. There are more towns like that abroad – I suppose Spoleto is a good example – towns which are more used and more compact than most of those here in England.

So that's the ideal I now have for a big show of mine. I love the thought of people just walking by and thinking, 'Oh, there's something over there, something watching.' Your sculpture is in the midst of life, but still has a certain unexpectedness – that's a nice relationship.

Frink's summary of her own position as an artist was characteristically clear-sighted, though perhaps unduly modest. Her remarks on the impact made by gender on her work are illuminating. They provide a very complete answer to feminist accusations that she was somehow a traitor to the cause because she refused to make any essential distinction between male and female artists.

The idea of things with a double nature has always been present in my work, because I don't feel that my work truly belongs to me. In a sense I've always been surprised to find myself working as an artist, because my family background and my childhood were so much removed from that kind of thing. I always find I'm split down the middle. On one side there is the creative person. On the other is someone – I wouldn't say conventional – but more straightforwardly practical. I enjoy my family, and domestic things like cooking. Perhaps that's because I'm a female. One thing I must have is a sense of order in my life. I divide myself between what I'm doing in the studio and what I'm doing elsewhere. I enjoy running a household and everything that goes with it – painting walls, moving furniture around, collecting funny stuff. I like to organise all that myself. I feel it's part of living.

137

I think a lot of women have sacrificed a great deal to become artists. They've felt they couldn't run a house at the same time, or have a family life — they've possibly avoided getting married. I've been very lucky in that I've had very happy times with my family. I don't resent the time that I give up to running a household because I enjoy it so much. I think a lot of other women artists find it difficult.

It was Elisabeth Frink's good fortune that she was able to integrate her preferred way of living so closely with the demands made by her work. It was her ill fortune that her career was so abruptly cut short when she still felt she had so much to do.

138